PARIS IN THE REVOLUTION

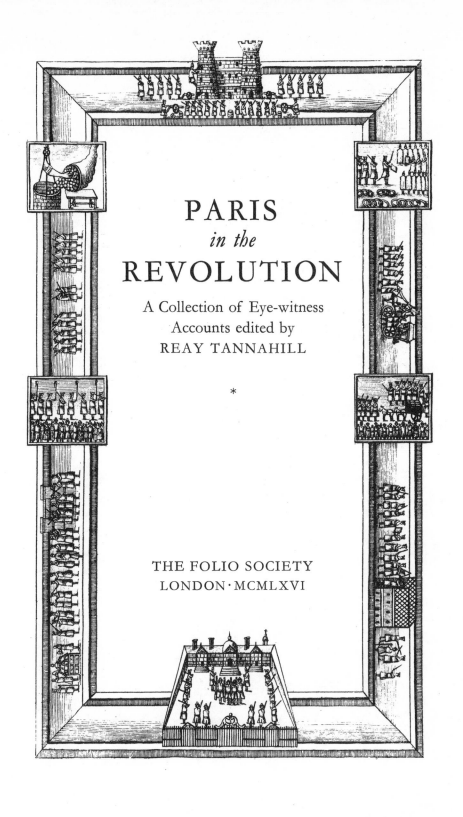

PARIS
in the
REVOLUTION

A Collection of Eye-witness
Accounts edited by
REAY TANNAHILL

*

THE FOLIO SOCIETY
LONDON · MCMLXVI

SECOND IMPRESSION 1967
Printed and bound in Great Britain
by Jarrold and Sons Limited, Norwich
Set in 12 point Garamond 2 points leaded

Contents

Introduction

Historians of the French revolution, said the poet Paul Valéry, spend their time bombarding one another with severed heads. It is a sobering thought. The bitter rivalries which arose between the leading figures of the revolutionary decade have not faded with the years. On the contrary, they have intensified. Robespierre, 'the sea-green incorruptible', was never hated as much by his contemporaries as he has been by later historians. Louis XVI is venerated as a martyr by men who would not have found a good word to say for him if he had lived. Danton, that great, vital, ugly bull of a man, is praised as 'tribune of the people' by zealots who see no inconsistency in his amassing a fortune while his 'people' rioted for bread.

To Frenchmen, the French revolution still offers a rich source of contention. But to the people of other countries, it is so clouded by myth that it has ceased to have much reality. Take one teaspoonful of French revolution, add a cupful of cliché, stir, and there is an instant-recognition symbol suitable for all tastes. For romantics, it is the first splendid expression of idealism in action. For royalists, it is the classic proof that mob rule ends in blood-stained anarchy. For politicians and military men, it is the beginning of the modern world. For schoolboys—and adults, too—it is *A Tale of Two Cities* and *The Scarlet Pimpernel*.

What was the French revolution really about? What did it mean to the people who were personally involved in it? What was it like to live in Paris at the time?—for according to one contemporary writer, it was Paris which made the revolution, and it was Paris which brought it to grief. *Paris in the Revolution* attempts to answer these questions by using the raw materials of history, the very words of people who took part and the graphic work of artists who were the forerunners of today's news-cameramen.

It is one of the charms of eighteenth-century literature that, although education had spread to a surprisingly wide cross-section of society, it had not yet spread widely enough to produce a standardized language or style. As a result, the personality of the author very often shines through his prose. In many of the reports quoted in the following pages, the eye-witnesses emerge as distinct individuals rather than as mere historical 'sources'. This not only adds spice to the narrative. It also gives the reader a chance to reach his own conclusions about the reliability of the witness. Listen, for example, to the Scots gardener, Thomas Blaikie, as he reproves a trigger-happy agitator so quellingly that the man slinks off with his tail between his legs—or, as

Blaikie puts it, 'slu[d]ges off very quietelly'. Or to Weber, the short-tempered Austrian who, unaware that the September massacres are taking place outside his very cell, tells the murderers' henchmen precisely what he thinks of their manners. Or to Madame Roland, whose comment on Danton—'I could not reconcile the idea of a good man with that face'—tells more about Madame Roland than it does about Danton.

As any lawyer or police officer will testify, however, eye-witness reports must be treated with reserve. Allowance must always be made for the prejudices of the witness and his degree of acquaintance with the subtleties of the situation. In most of the extracts which follow, the writer's prejudices are self-evident; where they are not, I have indicated them in the linking text. A further hazard in the case of the French revolution is to be found in the number of entirely fictitious 'eye-witness reports' which emerged in response to events; many myths have been perpetuated by the frequent repetition of such reports, which are as colourful and satisfying as they are untrustworthy. L.-S. Mercier, for example, that great chronicler of the Parisian scene at the end of the eighteenth century, has left a description of the execution of Robespierre in which the ring of truth is almost deafening. Unfortunately, Mercier was incarcerated in a prison cell at the time and it is difficult to see how he could have witnessed any of the events of that day, or indeed of any other day during the months before and after. Again, a lawyer named Maton de la Varenne published a hideous description of the September massacres, where he described the murderers dipping bread in the blood of their victims. Maton de la Varenne has long been discredited, but his story is often quoted— even today—as 'fact'. The reader will not find either of these episodes in the present book.

What might be called the history of the history of the revolution is a fascinating subject in its own right. Among the fifty thousand contemporary documents which are estimated to be in existence today, there are many other tales which sound as convincing as those of Mercier and Maton de la Varenne and which are just as apocryphal. Throughout the nineteenth century, there was a flood of 'hitherto unpublished' memoirs and diaries attributed to notable figures of the revolutionary era. Some of these were pure fiction. In other cases, the editors worked from original notes. Sometimes, eye-witnesses were interviewed by authors who had a particular end in mind. Rosalie Lamorlière's account of the last days of Marie Antoinette, for example (see page 86), was told by an illiterate maidservant to a biographer intent on rehabilitating the memory of that maligned queen. If his version of Rosalie's words had not been confirmed from other sources, one might easily have suspected him of refining and polishing the literal truth to the advantage of his own thesis.

Authentic diaries like that of Gouverneur Morris; letters, like those of Reichardt, which were published within months of being written; newspaper reports which appeared within days of the events they described; speeches in the Jacobin club, which were approved by the club for immediate publication; all these are reliable guides to what people felt at the time. After mid 1792, however, memoirs and reminiscences were subject to political pressures; as long as the reader recognizes these pressures, he will find they give added interest to the narrative.

During the Terror, for example, it was dangerous to be found in possession of anything that might be construed as anti-revolutionary. As a result, much material was destroyed; part of the memoirs which Madame Roland wrote in prison were consigned to the flames by the nervous custodian to whom she had entrusted them. Nor were things much easier after the fall of Robespierre. Then, ex-Robespierrists became intent on justifying their past misdeeds; to exculpate themselves, they hastened into print with claims that they had only done what they were told, and it was hardly their fault that their masters had been villains. The memoirs of Vilate (see page 95) belong in this category. During the Napoleonic empire, there was a certain amount of freedom as long as what was written did not glorify the First Republic or cast doubts on the emperor's right to rule. But when the restoration came, the Bourbons set about a full-scale purge of ex-revolutionaries. Apology and justification began once more. The testimony of the lawyer Chauveau-Lagarde (see page 88) is an example of this. In 1830, there was another revolution, and it became not only permissible but desirable to have taken part in the events of 1789–94. One can only feel sympathy for the authors involved. It must have been very muddling.

A list of detailed notes on the quotations used in this book will be found on page 117. Most of the French originals have been newly translated—not for the sake of it, but because, where translations already exist, they usually date from the Victorian era. Then, the French revolution was expected to produce delicious shivers down well-padded Victorian spines, and what has been described as the *catastrophe-horreur!* school of translation was much in favour. The results were often ludicrous and unconvincing, as well as actively misleading.

1] Louis XVI

Most of the illustrations in the present book can be dated to within a very few years of the events they show; some even more closely. The massacre at the Salpétrière Prison, for example, appeared as an illustration to a current periodical. The painting of the attack on the Tuileries (10 August 1792) was exhibited at the Paris Salon of 1793—strange though it may be to think of an annual art exhibition surviving throughout these agitated years. The portrait of Louis XVI (page 71) was done in the space of time between his trial and execution.

There are by no means as many contemporary illustrations as there are quotations. This is hardly to be wondered at; there were far fewer people who knew how to paint than people who knew how to write. Furthermore, when the wars began, a large number of artists set off patriotically for the frontiers. By late 1792, David's teaching studio was almost empty of pupils for this reason. Owners and artists were, however, less inclined to destroy a painting in haste than a manuscript record of events, or an engraving of which other copies existed. Somehow, too, a picture seemed less incriminating than words unless the subject was patently contrary to public policy.

Occasionally, of course, there were casualties. On 21 January 1794, the first anniversary of the king's execution, a government observer reported that, 'on the suspicion of there being in the rue St-Jacques printsellers who sold many engravings of the late king and queen, people went there and burned all the pictures'. A few artists were guillotined, but this was more for their political activities than for their art. Many of the men who guided the revolution were men of culture, firmly convinced that art must play an important role in the type of society they hoped to create. More immediately, they believed in it as propaganda, and were therefore much more inclined to forgive an artist his misdemeanours than other members of society.

The pre-eminent artist of the revolutionary period was Jacques-Louis David. David's early work was in the rococo style, but he deserted this in the 1780s for a neo-classicism more in tune with the spirit of the age. Many of his subjects are based on allegory or symbolism; Liberty, in the guise of a scantily clad young woman with her foot firmly planted on the image of despotism, is a characteristic motif. David's portraits and narrative paintings, however, are superb in their way (see illustrations nos. 4, 17, 36 and 52). They have a romantic grandeur which may bear limited relation to truth but which is immensely satisfying. His dramatic sense stood David in good stead for the propaganda pageants he produced. He was the Sam Goldwyn of the decade, turning the entire population of Paris into 'extras' for his crowd scenes on the great fête days of the revolution. Part of his own production script for the Fête of the Supreme Being is quoted on page 96. David, as well as being artistic dictator, was also one of the great teachers of his time, and his pupils included Gérard, Gros, and Ingres.

The narrative art of the revolution falls into four main categories. There are the heroic canvases devoted to outstanding events; there are wash drawings and sketches, sometimes done for their own sake, sometimes intended as preliminaries for a projected work in oils; there are detailed drawings made soon after the event and later engraved for publication; and there are popular prints, some triumphant, some satirical, many of them commissioned by the government from David and other artists 'to awaken the public spirit and show how atrocious and ridiculous are the enemies of liberty and the republic'. Inevitably, it was the topical prints that were most often destroyed, since by their very nature they were soon outdated—and yesterday's prints could be as dangerous as yesterday's opinions during the course of the revolutionary decade. Details of all the pictures reproduced in the present book are given in the notes on the illustrations, on page 123.

Just as long-discredited memoirs continue to be quoted, so the emotional judgements of past historians remain in common currency. *Was* there a wholesale slaughter of aristocrats during the years of revolution? Modern statistical surveys have shown that probably only one aristocrat in three hundred went to the guillotine. *Was* the Paris mob such a rabble as Taine described, composed entirely of the ugliest dregs of society? Recent research suggests that by far the largest element consisted of artisans, small shop-keepers, and craftsmen of the luxury trades—jewellers, wigmakers, coach-builders, servants to the nobility—thrown out of work by the flight of many of their aristocratic customers, and kept out of work by public disapproval of the conspicuous waste which their trades represented. It has been shown, too, that when 'the rabble' broke into shops in search of goods in short supply or available only at inflated prices, they very frequently paid for what they took —even if the sum they paid was what they estimated the goods to be worth rather than what the shopkeeper asked for them. Similarly, robberies and housebreaking were rare, and when, after the battle at the Tuileries in 1792, a member of 'the rabble' was found looting, he was summarily executed by his fellows.

Was the revolution the saga of blood and flame which Carlyle's imagination depicted? That is something every reader must judge for himself. Certainly, there was blood. As the blade of the guillotine thudded relentlessly into its niche, the blood seemed to flow in torrents. But it was only in August 1792, three years after the revolution began, that the guillotine was first used to behead a political prisoner. It is salutary to reflect that before 1789 only men of noble birth had the right to be beheaded, and that execution by decapitation was therefore a sign of the equality for all which the revolution had brought about. The guillotine itself was first developed by the revolutionaries from the best of motives; methods of carrying out the death penalty had been carefully investigated by the medical authorities of the time, and the conclusion had been reached that this was the only satisfactory way of executing a man without inflicting unnecessary pain. 'The law exacts justice, not vengeance.' It is one of the ironies of history that a machine developed for such reasons should have made multiple executions both psychologically and technically possible. If an executioner with a sword or axe had had to carry out the task of beheading, the Terror would perhaps never have taken place. No crowd could have tolerated the sight of hundreds of heads laboriously hacked off. No executioner, needing a new edge to his blade for every client, could have matched the guillotine's record of twenty-one heads in thirty-six minutes.

Blood was shed by the guillotine after a due process of law, however arbitrary that process might sometimes be. Otherwise, very little flowed in Paris except under the emotional pressure of events, as in August and September 1792. Outside Paris, bloodshed was mainly confined to areas where there was civil unrest or violent counter-revolutionary activity, or where, as in the frontier provinces, a state of emergency existed. In other parts of the country, the guillotine might claim only one victim in six months.

So much for the blood. What of the flame? There was, in fact, surprisingly little destruction during the revolution. A few statues of past despots were hurled down. The Bastille, that symbol of old hatreds, was dismantled stone by stone. A number of houses or châteaux were burned or sacked. But the revolutionaries were more concerned with renaming streets and squares (to the infinite confusion of the populace) than with demolishing buildings whose elegance they admired.

Who were these revolutionaries, these 'monsters' who held twenty-five million Frenchmen in subjection? Their personalities will begin to emerge in the pages that follow. But it is worth saying here that those who figured in the history of the revolution were young men; it is worth remembering that— even in an age when normal life expectancy was low—Louis XVI, who had ruled France for almost twenty years, was not yet forty when he went to the guillotine in 1793. Robespierre was only thirty-five when he died, Danton thirty-four, and Saint-Just a mere twenty-six.

At the beginning, the young men had their ideals, and these were given partial expression in the Declaration of the Rights of Man. But ideals were soon tempered by reality, and the realities of France in 1789 were of frightening complexity. If a new government taking power in Britain in the year 1964 —a government composed of men who had been preparing for the event for thirteen years, in a country where the 'secrets' of finance, administration, negotiation and civil control are all public knowledge, and where a considerable degree of social regulation exists—could complain that the country's economic situation was worse than they had realized, consider the problems that faced the men of eighteenth-century France. Of such matters they knew next to nothing. Even if they had had to start from scratch, their problems would have been bad enough. As it was, they also had to disentangle an economic situation which would have given even modern administrators many a sleepless night, an economic situation which had driven Louis XVI to call the States-General into session for the first time in a hundred and seventy-five years. Even to cut the Gordian knot solved nothing. Of all the tragedies of 1789-94, this was perhaps the greatest: that the idealists of the revolution saw their own ideals gradually corroded by the relentless progress of events they could not control, until, in spite of all their brave hopes, they had no choice but to live for the moment—or die for it.

What, finally, was the background to the revolution? What brought it about?

Fundamentally, it was a product of the eighteenth-century situation, of the social changes which were taking place to a greater or lesser degree throughout the whole of Europe. In seventeenth-century France, it had been possible for an absolute monarch to carry the nation alone. But when Louis XIV died and was succeeded by lesser men, the burden slipped imperceptibly from the shoulders of the king and his ministers on to those of the emerging middle classes. By the late eighteenth century, these middle classes—many of them well educated, comfortably off, indoctrinated with the intellectual attitudes of the Century of Enlightenment—were wholly dissatisfied with the inferior position they occupied in relation to the aristocracy and the dignitaries of the church. Nevertheless, change might have come about by a gradual process, as it did elsewhere, had it not been for the miscalculations of the aristocracy. As Robespierre was to admit: 'In France, the judiciary, the nobles, the clergy, the wealthy, gave the revolution its original impetus. The people appeared on the scene only at a later stage. Those who gave the first impulse have long since repented, or at least wanted to put a stop to the revolution when they saw that the people might regain its sovereignty. But it was they who began it. Without their resistance and their miscalculations, the nation would still be under the yoke of despotism.'

Long wars, public and private extravagance, weak kings, ministers without enough authority to follow coherent policies, a restive aristocracy anxious to regain the political power of which it had been deprived by Louis XIV—all these had reduced the country to a state of economic chaos. Necker, the Genevan banker who was in charge of French finances from 1776 until 1781

A fête by night at the Petit Trianon; court life before the Revolution

and for other brief periods thereafter, was a genius at raising loans, and managed to keep the nation afloat for some time by this means—which ensured, of course, that when the crash came it would be even greater. By August 1786 Necker's successor, Calonne, had exhausted the loan market. He therefore proposed a general land tax, from which not even the aristocracy would be exempt. Since most members of the aristocracy were themselves comprehensively in debt, it was hardly to be supposed that this idea would meet with approval. Calonne fell, to be succeeded by Loménie de Brienne. Brienne presented very similar proposals to the *parlements*, the ancient bodies of magistrates whose duty was to register edicts, but who also had the right to remonstrate against the laws in Paris and certain provincial towns. The *parlements* rejected the proposals and demanded that the States-General be summoned.

This suited the aristocracy very well. According to tradition, the States-

General consisted of three elected bodies, one representing the clergy, one the aristocracy, and one 'the people'. When the States-General voted, it voted not by head, but as three separate units. Since the clergy was dominated by aristocrats who held high church office as a reward for services rendered, the first two estates were always certain to outvote the third.

When the facts of this situation dawned on the Third Estate—who had at first believed that, when the clergy, the aristocracy and the *parlements* spoke of 'the nation', they meant the nation rather than just its privileged élite—they reacted with speed and determination. During the last months of 1788, a verbal battle raged throughout France. The unprivileged classes suddenly found an identity of belief, a common cause against the masters who ruled them not because of talent but by the mere accident of birth. *What is the Third Estate?* demanded the Abbé Sieyès in his famous pamphlet. And replied: 'It is everything. What has it been in the political order until now? Nothing. What does it want? To become something.'

When the States-General met in May 1789, the Third Estate had gained one point. Its representation was to be double that of either of the other two estates. But the voting was still to be by estate, not by head. The battle over that point was yet to be fought, and it was to be the first battle of the French revolution.

Paris in the Revolution

The States-General

On 5 May 1789, the States-General met at Versailles for the first time since 1614. Protocol for the 1789 meeting was firmly based on the precedent of 1614, and the Third Estate—which was to be received by the king in a different manner from the other two—was required to present itself in its 'customary' garb of sober black, and was to remain with heads uncovered even when the king, the nobles and the clergy donned their hats. Mr Gouverneur Morris, statesman of the new American republic, was present on the occasion.

An old man who refused to dress in the costume prescribed for the Tiers [Third Estate] and who appears in his farmer's habit, receives a long and loud plaudit. Mr de Mirabeau is hissed, tho' not very loudly. The king at length arrives and takes his seat, the queen on his left, two steps lower than him. He makes a short speech, very proper and well spoken, or rather read. The tone and manner have all the *fierté* which can be desired or expected from the blood of the Bourbons. He is interrupted in the reading by acclamations so warm and of such lively affection that the tears start from my eyes in spite of myself. The queen weeps or seems to weep but not one voice is heard to wish her well. I would certainly raise mine if I were a Frenchman, but I have no right to express a sentiment and in vain solicit those who are near me to do it. After the king has spoken he takes off his hat, and when he puts it on again his nobles imitate the example. Some of the Tiers do the same, but by degrees they one after the other take them off again. The king then takes off *his* hat. The queen seems to think it wrong and a conversation seems to pass in which the king tells her he chuses to do it, whether consistent or not consistent with the ceremonial; but I would not swear to this, being too far distant to see very distinctly, much less to hear. The nobles uncover by degrees, so that if the ceremonial requires these manœuvres the troops are not yet properly drilled.

After the king's speech, and the coverings and uncoverings, the *Garde des Sceaux* [Keeper of the Seals] makes one much longer, but it is delivered in a very ungraceful manner and so indistinctly that nothing can be judged of it by me until it is in print. When he has done, Mr Necker rises. He tries to play the orator but he plays it very ill. The audience salute him with a long and loud plaudit. Animated by this approbation, he falls into action and emphasis, but a bad accent and an ungraceful manner destroy much of the effect which ought to follow from a composition written by Mr Necker and spoken by Mr Necker. He presently asks the king's leave to employ a clerk, which being granted the clerk proceeds in the lecture. It is very long [more than three hours]. It contains much information and many things very fine but it is too long, has many repetitions and too much compliment and what the French call *emphase*.

The plaudits were loud, long and incessant. These will convince the king and queen of the national sentiment and tend to prevent the effects of the [court] intrigue against the present administration, at least for a while. After this speech is over the king rises to depart and receives a long and affecting 'Vive le roi!' The queen rises, and to my great satisfaction she hears for the first time in several months the sound of 'Vive la reine!' She makes a low curtesy and this produces a louder acclamation, and that a lower curtesy.

But the general benevolence of this first day did not last for very long. Necker's speech, when divested of its 'action and emphasis' and complexity, turned out to contain the information that the three estates were still to vote as estates, not by head. The king had, in fact, given in to the nobles and clergy, and the Third Estate was relegated to the position of a powerless minority. It refused, however, to accept the situation. It embarked on a policy of non-cooperation. When this failed to make any impression, it adopted the title of National Assembly. This implied that the Third Estate represented the nation, that the Third Estate was all and the nobles and clergy nothing. It became clear that the king would have to take some action, and a royal session was called. The hall

3] Opening of the States-General in May 17

used by the Third Estate was closed down in preparation for this, and a guard was put on the doors. True to tradition, no one bothered to give the commoners a proper explanation of the circumstances and, in the state of tension which then existed, the deputies leapt to the conclusion that the 'National Assembly' was being forcibly closed down. Jean-Sylvain Bailly, president of the assembly, described what happened then.

In the avenue we met a great number of deputies. All were of the opinion that the assembly must meet and deliberate at such a delicate juncture, and that we must look for a suitable place. M Guillotin proposed the tennis court and we resolved upon going there. I walked at the head of the crowd of deputies and, fearing that some reason of policy might lead to its being closed to us, I asked five or six deputies to go ahead and make sure of it. The master of the tennis court received us with delight, and hastened to provide for us as best he could. . . .

There, then, was the National Assembly of France in a tennis court, in a place which had been witness to games and sport, and which was now to witness the destinies of the empire; in a place where the walls were dingy and bare, where there was not a seat to sit on. I was offered a chair. I rejected it. I could not be seated in front of an assembly which had to stand. I remained thus the whole of that laborious day. Throughout the sitting, we had only five or six benches and a table for writing on, but the place gained in dignity from the majesty it contained—the galleries filled with spectators, the crowd which gathered round the door and in the streets to a great distance, everything proclaimed that it was the nation which honoured a tennis court with its presence.

. . . As soon as the assembly was able to constitute itself and silence was obtained, I communicated the two letters which I had received from M de Brèze [the court master of ceremonies] and all the steps the secretaries and I had taken. Our conduct of the business was unanimously approved. The assembly thought that a letter from the grand master of ceremonies was not enough, and that there should have been a letter from the king himself to the president of the assembly, making his intentions known to him directly. After all, when the king had something to make known to the *parlement*, he wrote to the president; he wrote to the archbishop of Paris concerning matters of piety. Even in such early days, the assembly could ask to be treated at least like the *parlement*. . . . The question of whether the king had the right to suspend the sittings of the assembly was not openly discussed, but the feeling was that it would be very dangerous for the king to have that right. It was felt that sittings could not be suspended, at least in that fashion. . . . It was necessary to occupy ourselves with the means of preventing a repetition of such events. Tempers became heated; some deputies went to extremes and were of the opinion that the assembly should transfer its sitting to Paris and depart forthwith, on foot, and in a body. One member wrote out a motion on the subject. All would have been lost if such an extreme measure had been taken. A cavalry squadron might well have been sent to halt the march; at the very least, the assembly would have cut itself off from the king, and such a step would have had far-reaching consequences. If the motion had been put, it was to be feared that the excitement of the moment might have led to its being adopted by acclamation and without consideration. But another member had the idea of the oath.

A general shout of approval immediately went up; and after a comparatively short discussion the assembly took the following resolution, so simple, but so firm:

> The National Assembly, taking into consideration that, called to settle the constitution of the kingdom, to bring about the regeneration of public order, and to maintain the true principles of the monarchy, nothing can prevent it from carrying on with its deliberations in whatever place it may be forced to establish itself, and that, in short, wherever its members are gathered, there is the National Assembly,

4] Bailly administers the Oath of the Tennis Court, 20 June 17

resolves that all members of this assembly will immediately take a solemn oath never to break up and to meet wherever circumstances dictate, until the constitution of the kingdom is established and consolidated on firm foundations; and that the said oath having been taken, each and every member will confirm by his signature this unshakeable resolution.

The resolution agreed, I asked in my capacity of president to be first to take the oath . . . then the whole assembly took it under my guidance. I pronounced the form in a voice so loud and clear that my words were heard by all the people who were in the street, and immediately, amid cheers, there rose from the assembly and from the crowd of citizens outside repeated and universal cries of 'Vive le roi!'

The assembly, in its firm and courageous conduct, even if it took useful precautions against the minister, even if it armed itself against despotism, was thus demonstrably united in heart and spirit with the king, and had no intention of doing anything against his legitimate authority. It even made a point of declaring in its resolution that one of its duties was to maintain the true principles of the monarchy, so as to prove to all that, whatever was hostile in its proceedings, was directed against despotism and not against the monarchy.

For ten days, the king veered with whichever wind blew strongest at the moment. Finally, after half the clergy and just under twenty per cent of the nobles had voluntarily gone over to the National Assembly, the wind of change prevailed. The king instructed the two privileged orders to join the Third Estate. They did so, in bitter silence, on 30 June 1789.

The Bastille Falls

Violent activity on the part of journalists and pamphleteers was one of the first visible signs of change in the early days of the French revolution. Orators and agitators, too, were busy in the gardens and coffee-houses of the Palais Royal, encouraged by the man who would succeed to the throne if the house of Bourbon fell. This was Philippe, Duc d'Orléans, later known as Philippe-Égalité.

In June 1789, the English traveller Arthur Young found himself in Paris.

I went to the Palais Royal to see what new things were published, and to procure a catalogue of all. Every hour produces something new. Thirteen came out today, sixteen yesterday and ninety-two last week. We think sometimes that Debrett's or Stockdale's shops at London are crowded, but they are mere deserts compared to Desein's and some others here, in which one can scarcely squeeze from the door to the counter. The price of printing two years ago was from 27 livres to 30 livres per sheet, but now it is from 60 livres to 80 livres.

This spirit of reading political tracts, they say, spreads into the provinces so that all the presses of France are equally employed. Nineteen-twentieths of these productions are in favour of liberty, and commonly violent against the

5] New pamphlets and journals poured from the presses

clergy and nobility; I have today bespoke many of this description that have reputation; but inquiring for such as had appeared on the other side of the question, to my astonishment I find there are but two or three that have merit enough to be known. Is it not wonderful that, while the press teems with the most levelling and even seditious principles, that if put in execution would over-turn the monarchy, nothing in reply appears, and not the least step is taken by the court to restrain this extreme licentiousness of publication? It is easy to conceive the spirit that must thus be raised among the people.

But the coffee-houses in the Palais Royal present yet more singular and astonishing spectacles; they are not only crowded within, but other expectant crowds are at the doors and windows, listening *à gorge deployé* to certain orators, who from chairs or tables harangue each his little audience. The eagerness with which they are heard, and the thunder of applause they receive for every sentiment of more than common hardiness or violence against the present government, cannot easily be imagined.

The atmosphere of unease spread by the pamphleteers and orators was intensified by the fact that the court had summoned up 20,000 troops from the provinces. The climax came when the court party felt itself strong enough to dismiss Necker, whom the people —for no good reason—idolized. They may still have believed that that persuasive financier might be able to do something about the price of bread; in 1789, a four-pound loaf cost 14½ sous, and the effective daily wage of, say, a builder's labourer was only 18 sous. All these irritants combined to persuade the ordinary people of Paris that they were about to be crushed under the scarlet heels of the aristocrats, just when they had thought they were on the threshold of freedom. It was too much. They set off to look for arms to protect themselves. Some they found in a raid on the Hôtel des Invalides; but they needed powder and ammunition, too, and it was rumoured that there were vast stocks of powder in that most hated of prisons, the Bastille.

According to Lord Dorset, Britain's special ambassador in France:

A large detachment with two pieces of cannon went to the Bastille to demand the ammunition that was there, the *Gardes Bourgeoises* [the citizens' militia formed the day before] not being then sufficiently provided: a flag of truce was sent on before and was answered from within, notwithstanding which the governor (the Marquis de Launay), contrary to all precedent, fired upon the people and killed several. This proceeding so enraged the populace that they rushed to the very gates with a determination to force their way through if possible. Upon this, the governor agreed to let in a certain number of them on condition that they should not commit any violence. These terms being acceded to, a detachment of about forty in number advanced and were admitted, but the drawbridge was immediately drawn up again and the whole party instantly massacred. This breach of honour aggravated by so glaring an act of inhumanity excited a spirit of revenge and tumult such as might naturally be expected. The two pieces of cannon were immediately placed against the gate and very soon made a breach which, with the disaffection that as is supposed prevailed within, produced a sudden surrender of that fortress.

Lord Dorset's account is, near enough, the account of events which was current throughout Paris. No one—least of all M de Launay himself, or the besiegers—

really knew what was going on. Later analysis showed that Lord Dorset's account was wrong in many respects, but it was what the people believed at the time, and that was what mattered in this, the first mass upsurge of the French revolution. To be known as one of the 'conquerors of the Bastille' soon became an epithet of honour. One such, Jean-Baptiste Humbert, issued a pamphlet containing his own account of the event. When he reached the Bastille, from the Invalides:

It was about half past three; the first bridge was lowered, the chains severed. But the portcullis barred the way; people were engaged in getting the cannon in by hand, having unlimbered them first. I crossed by the little bridge and helped on the inside to get the two pieces of cannon in. When they were remounted on their carriages, with one voluntary accord we formed up in ranks of five or six and I found myself in the first rank.

Thus formed up, we marched as far as the drawbridge of the château; there, I saw two slain soldiers, stretched out on either side. On the left, where I was, the dead soldier's uniform was of the Vintimille. I could not make out the uniform of the soldier stretched out on the right.

The cannons were levelled; the bronze one opposite the large drawbridge, and the little iron one damascened in silver, opposite the little bridge. This cannon forced me to leave my place, and as we wanted at that moment to know if, on the turret, someone might be making some new sign of amnesty, I gave myself the task of running across the earthwork to look.

During this mission, they decided to begin the attack with musket fire. I hurried to get back to my post, but my way being barred by a crowd of people —in spite of the danger—I had, in order to reach it again, to return by the parapet; I was even obliged to step on the corpse of the soldier of Vintimille.

We each fired about six shots.

In the meantime, the governor of the Bastille was finding his troops mutinous. One of the defenders continues the story:

About four o'clock in the evening, the governor, urged by the under-officers to surrender the Bastille, seeing himself that he could not long sustain the siege without provisions, seized the match from one of the cannon in the inner court in order to set a light to the powder in the Tour de la Liberté, which would have inevitably blown up part of the Faubourg St-Antoine and all the houses near the Bastille, if two under-officers had not prevented him from carrying out his intention. They made him withdraw at the point of the bayonet. Ferrand forced the governor away from the gun store and when he then went down to the Tour de la Liberté he was similarly repulsed by Bequard.

It was then that M de Launay asked the garrison what course he was to take, that he saw nothing else for it but to blow himself up rather than expose himself to being butchered by the people, whose frenzy could not be escaped; that it was necessary to go up again to the towers, continue to fight, and blow ourselves up sooner than surrender.

The soldiers replied that it was impossible to fight much longer, that they would resign themselves to anything rather than cause a great number of citizens to perish, that it was more expedient to send the drum up on the towers to sound the recall, to hoist a white flag, and to capitulate. The governor, having no flag, gave a white handkerchief. . . .

The Swiss officer spoke to them [the besiegers] through a kind of loop-hole close to the drawbridge and asked them to retire with the honours of war. They answered no. The officer wrote out the capitulation and passed it through the same hole, saying that we would like very much to yield and lay

M. de Launay seized after the fall of the Bastille, 14 July 1789

down our arms, if it was promised that the soldiers would not be massacred. They began to shout: 'Lower your bridge; nothing will happen to you.'

It was on this promise that the governor gave the key of the little draw-bridge which he had in his pocket to Gaiard, corporal, and Pereau, under-officer, who opened the gate and lowered the bridge. . . . It is easy to see that the Bastille was not taken by assault. No breach was made. We defy anyone to prove there was; entry was made when we lowered the bridge.

That same evening, an English physician, Edward Rigby, was in the rue St Honoré. There was an immense crowd.

We saw a flag, some large keys, and a paper elevated on a pole above the crowd in which was inscribed 'La Bastille est prise et les portes sont ouvertes.' The intelligence of this extraordinary event, thus communicated, produced an impression upon the crowd really indescribable. A sudden burst of the most frantic joy instantaneously took place; every possible mode in which the most rapturous feelings of joy could be expressed, were everywhere exhibited. Shouts and shrieks, leaping and embracing, laughter and tears, every sound and every gesture, including even what approached to nervous and hysterical affection, manifested, among the promiscuous crowd, such an instantaneous and unanimous emotion of extreme gladness as I should suppose was never before experienced by human beings. . . .

The crowd passed on to the Palais Royal, and in a few minutes another succeeded. Its approach was also announced by loud and triumphant acclamations, but, as it came nearer, we soon perceived a different character, as though bearing additional testimony to the fact reported by the first crowd, the impression by it on the people was of a very different kind. A deep and hollow murmur at once pervaded them, their countenances expressing amazement mingled with alarm. We could not at first explain these circum-stances; but as we pressed more to the centre of the crowd we suddenly partook of the general sensation, for we then, and not till then, perceived two bloody heads raised on pikes, which were said to be the heads of the Marquis de Launay, governor of the Bastille, and of Monsieur Flesselles, *Prévôt des Marchands* [a member of the municipal authority, who had tried to prevent the people from arming themselves]. It was a chilling and a horrid sight! An idea of savageness and ferocity was impressed on the spectators, and instantly checked those emotions of joy which had before prevailed. Many others, as well as ourselves, shocked and disgusted at this scene, retired immediately from the streets.

Of the authorities, Louis XVI was the least concerned over the fall of the Bastille.

Clothed in the impenetrable armour of the divine right of kings—and, more specifically, the divine right of the Bourbons—he regarded the whole matter as merely another in the series of bread riots which had scarred the history of the eighteenth century. A riot over the price of bread and the dismissal of M Necker? Very well, calm the people by recalling M Necker. The king was to treat most of the events of the next three years on this same day-to-day basis. Only in the last few months of his life, perhaps, did he come to realize that his people regarded him, not as a god, but as a man. And even then he could not bring himself to believe that they might be right.

Others were less phlegmatic. The day after the Bastille fell, the privileged classes began to leave Paris and France. Within two months, 20,000 passports were issued.

The deputies of the Third Estate, too, were worried. Most of them were comfortable, conservative citizens whose interest in liberty—decked out though it might be in fine words and idealistic phrases—went no further than ensuring for themselves a place in that hierarchy from which they had previously been barred. Rioting was a threat to property and, as such, could not be tolerated.

The October Days

In Paris, a new city authority had constituted itself at the Hôtel de Ville. It consisted of the secondary electors who had met originally to elect the Paris delegates to the Third Estate of the States-General. The new mayor was Bailly, who had presided over the Oath of the Tennis Court. The day after the Bastille fell, the spontaneously founded garde *or* milice bourgeoise *was given official recognition as the National Guard and placed under the command of General de La Fayette, the young French nobleman who had become a hero of the American War of Independence.*

Thus the Third Estate took over local as well as national government. But Paris remained in a state of ferment. The States-General—which had now become the 'Constituent Assembly' and was engaged in drawing up a suitable constitution for the country —seemed to do little but make speeches. Their sentiments were impeccable. Nothing could have been more commendable than the Declaration of the Rights of Man; nothing more desirable than the renunciation of aristocratic privileges. Nothing, that is, but a more plentiful supply of bread, an increase in wages, and a decrease in the growing number of unemployed. Some revolutionary newspapers suggested that matters would not improve until the king came back to live in Paris, among his people. This opinion was also held by a number of politicians, who felt that the king might be more amenable in such a situation. The Orléanist faction was delighted to help trouble the waters so that they might fish in them. The situation finally erupted when it was rumoured that, at a banquet of the king's bodyguard at Versailles, the national cockade had been trampled underfoot.

On 5 October, Stanislas Maillard—one of the 'conquerors of the Bastille'—went in the course of his duties to the Hôtel de Ville.

It was occupied by a multitude of women who wanted no men amongst them and kept on saying that the Ville [municipal authority] was made up of aristocrats, that I must be one of them because I was dressed in black, and that they refused to let me in, which obliged me to set off to change my coat. But going down the steps of the Hôtel de Ville I was stopped by five or six women who made me go back up, shouting to all the others that I was a volunteer of the Bastille and that there was nothing to be feared from me. Then, having got in amongst them, I found some of them breaking in the doors below, others rooting out papers in the offices, saying that this was all anyone had done since the beginning of the revolution and that they would burn them.

I begged them to calm down, with the assistance of one Richard Dupin. The women repeated that the men had not enough guts to revenge themselves, and that they would give a better account of themselves than the men. At a moment when I was at the far end of the courtyard, turning round I saw a number of men coming up, armed with pikes, cudgels, pitchforks, and other weapons, who had forced the women to let them enter. They threw themselves on the doors the women had begun battering at, and broke them down with the help of the big hammers they had and crowbars that they found in the Hôtel de Ville. They took all the arms they found and gave them to the women.

After a brush with two women who proposed setting a light to all the papers in the Hôtel de Ville, Maillard suggested they should form a deputation to the municipal authority and explain the bread situation. But they replied that 'the entire Commune was composed of bad citizens who all deserved to be hanged, Messieurs Bailly and La Fayette first'. Maillard concluded that the only solution was to march the women off to Versailles; by the time they had covered twelve miles on foot, he argued, the authorities would have had time to do something to control the situation. After some disorders, the column set off. They had a slight scuffle with the solitary Swiss guard on duty in the gardens of the Tuileries, but Maillard's flock arrived at the Champs Élysées in good order. Here, they were joined by others.

I saw arriving from all directions detachments of women armed with broomsticks, cudgels, pitchforks, swords, pistols, and muskets without however any of them having ammunition, so that they proposed to make me go with a detachment of them to look for powder at the Arsenal. But I made use of the order I had from M Gouvion [which permitted Maillard to draw

7] Hungry, wet, and bad-tempered, the women of Paris march to Versailles

ammunition for the military volunteers normally under his command] and showed it to them, pretending that this order had been given for them but that there was no powder at the Arsenal (although I really knew there was), and saying I thought it prudent that, as they only wanted to go to the National Assembly to demand justice and bread, they should go without arms, and that they would move the assembly more by presenting themselves without arms than by using force. Thanks to my prayers and protestations, I succeeded in making the women lay down their arms, except for some who refused. But the wiser ones made them give in. . . .

I had acquired the confidence of the women to such an extent that they all said with one voice that they would not have anyone else but me at their head. A score broke away to line up the men behind them, and we took the road to Versailles with eight or ten drums before us. The women then could be numbered at about six or seven thousand.

We went by Chaillot along the river. All the houses were closed up, in fear, no doubt, of pilfering. The women, in spite of that, went and knocked on every door and when someone refused to open, they wanted to break it down. . . . Seeing this, and wanting to prevent the ruin of the inhabitants, I called a halt and told the women that they would do themselves no good by carrying on this way, and that people would look on their actions unfavourably, whereas if they went peaceably, with decorum, all the citizens of the capital would be grateful to them for it. They gave in at last to my arguments and advice and continued on their way soberly until Sèvres, although on this part of the journey they stopped ten court messengers and carriages who were going to Versailles, in case, they said, someone might close the bridge at Sèvres to prevent them crossing. They did no harm to these people.

Outside Sèvres, Maillard called a halt and, hearing that all the shops and taverns were closed, sent eight armed men off to see what the bakers could be persuaded to provide. All the men could find were eight four-pound loaves. When Maillard told the women this, it

raised murmurs among them and led them to split into groups to think up and plan action, which made me fear for the inhabitants of Sèvres. I thought it my duty to call the women back into line. A great number obeyed, but others remained behind, which made me think they were determined to cause trouble. I decided to use the influence of those who seemed agreeable and sent them to join the groups of the others and inspire them to a different way of thinking from the one I was told they had. But they could make no headway and soon the groups dispersed and the women went off to all the doors and shops of wine merchants, innkeepers, lemonade sellers, and other citizens. They even went into a courtyard, took benches and other pieces of wood, and set about breaking down the doors and pulling down all the merchants' signs.

Maillard, however, managed to find some wine for the women, and they proceeded on their march to Versailles with little other incident. When they arrived at the National Assembly, Maillard and a small group of women demanded bread for Paris, and the punishment of the guards who had insulted the national cockade. The response of the National Assembly and of the king—when he returned from hunting—seemed satisfactory, and the Parisians settled down in Versailles where they spent a quiet night. La Fayette and the National Guard, who had set out in belated pursuit, found Versailles apparently quiet when they arrived. At daybreak next morning, however, according to the newspaper Révolutions de Paris:

The people scattered out in the streets; they saw one of the bodyguard at a window in the right wing of the château, they provoked him, they taunted him; the madman loads his musket, fires, and kills the son of a Parisian saddler, soldier of the National Guard; immediately the people burst into the château, search for the culprit, think they recognize him; one of the bodyguard is dragged to the foot of the staircase in the marble courtyard; his head is cut off; it is put on the end of a pike [a Parisian custom of pre-revolutionary days] and carried to Paris with that of one of the bodyguard killed the previous evening. . . . The people had stopped other members of the bodyguard in various parts of the château, and proposed to punish all for the fault of one, the death of the National Guardsman. One is massacred with stabs of a pike, while he is trying to calm the people; another has his head cut off by a National Guardsman whom the madmen force to this cruel task; they break into, they ransack the headquarters of the bodyguard, and at the same time search for them in every corner of the château, even in the apartments of the king himself.

But the king's apartment was full of National Guards. La Fayette arrived and, according to his own account (written in the third person),
from the balcony heatedly and even violently harangued the multitude who filled the marble courtyard, and when the king and his family, after having promised to come to Paris, withdrew from the balcony: 'Madame,' said he to the queen, 'what is your personal intention?' 'I know the fate which awaits me,' she replied nobly. 'But my duty is to die at the feet of the king and in the arms of my children.' 'Very well, madame, come with me.' 'What! Alone on the balcony? Did you not see the gestures they made at me?' And, in truth, they had been horrible. 'Yes, madame. Let us go.' And appearing with her, in face of those waves which still roared in the middle of a cordon of National Guards who occupied the three sides of the courtyard but could not quell the centre of it, La Fayette—unable to make himself heard—had recourse to a gesture which was hazardous but decisive; he kissed the queen's hand. The multitude, struck by this act, cried: 'Vive le général! Vive la reine!' The king, who had remained a few paces behind, came on to the balcony and said, in tones of emotion and gratitude: 'Now what can you do for my guards?' 'Bring me one,' replied La Fayette; then giving his cockade to this body-guard, he embraced him, and the people shouted: 'Vive le garde du corps!' From that moment, peace was restored.

The king, the queen and the royal children returned to Paris, accompanied by a rowdy escort of their subjects. A Scots gardener and botanist, Thomas Blaikie, who lived most of his later life in France, was offended to the depths of his soul by the sight.

The scene was most shocking to see, the poissards [fish-wives] mounted up on the cannon, some with one of the gards coats or hatts, and the poor gardes

8] The heads of the two bodyguards brought back from Versailles

obliged to be conducted along with them in this manner and the heads of their comerades that was killed at Versailles brought along with them. The king and queen and dauphin was likewise conducted in this humiliating condition; the maire of Paris was at the Barriere des Bonnes hommes below Passy to receive them and, as a form, to present the keys of the town to the king—which might be looked upon rather as a mockery than otherwise. The people was all roaring out 'Voilà le boulanger et la boulangère et le petit mitron', saying that now they should have bread as they now had got the baker and his wife and boy. The queen sat at the bottom on the coach with the dauphin on her knees in this condition, while some of the blackguards in the rable was firing there guns over her head.

As I stood by the coach, one man fired and loaded his gun four times and fired it over the queen's head. I told him to desiste but he said he would continue, but when I told him I should try by force to stop him and not have people hurt by his imprudence, some cryed it was right and so he sluged off very quietelly; and after the corte went on they lodged the king and his family in the thuilleries.

Interlude

'The baker and his wife and boy' had been brought back to Paris, and the assembly soon followed. The representatives of the people thought *they had won, but their attitude towards the problem of government was, to say the least, ambivalent. They believed that they were now the masters, but still felt that the process of governing was a matter for the king and his ministers. They were delighted to interfere in this process, but quite unequipped to take control of it themselves. Instead, they devoted themselves to two major tasks. The first was to create a constitution; they took two years to produce it, and it was a dead letter within a year of its completion. The second task was to raise money. Here the agile brain of the Bishop of Autun, better known to history as Talleyrand, provided a quicker solution. He suggested that church property be nationalized in return for the state's taking over financial responsibility for the ecclesiastical establishment. Assignats— paper money backed by the profits on the sale of church lands—were in circulation by 1790; they were to be one of the primary factors in an economic inflation which kept France on the boil for the next ten years.*

The politicians might not be sure of their power, but ordinary people thought the revolution was over. The first anniversary of Bastille day provided an occasion for national festivities. 'Trees of liberty' were planted all over the country, and innumerable fêtes were held. At first it seemed as if the preparations for the Paris fête were not

The people's representatives, planting a symbolic tree of liberty

going to be completed in time; as a result, half the population turned out the night before to lend a hand. Camille Desmoulins described the scene in his journal, Révolutions de France et de Brabant.

Fifteen thousand workers labour at the Champ-de-Mars. The rumour spreads that they cannot hasten the work enough. Soon a swarm of 150,000 others rushes up and the field is transformed into a workshop nine hundred yards long. It is the workshop of Paris, of all Paris; whole families, whole public bodies, whole districts flock there. They come up three by three, with a pick or spade on their shoulder, singing all together the well-known refrain of a new song: 'Ça ira, ça ira!' Yes, 'Ça ira!' repeat those who hear them. . . . A child from Vincennes, asked if he is enjoying the work, replies that he cannot yet offer the country more than his sweat, but he offers that with great pleasure. . . . The printers had inscribed on their flag: 'Printing, first torch of liberty'; those of M Prud'homme [proprietor of the journal *Révolutions de Paris*] wore bonnets of the same paper as is used to bind the *Révolutions*; written on them was 'Révolutions de Paris'. I must not forget the street-vendors; wanting to go one better than other bodies, and with public well-being very much at heart, they had agreed to consecrate a whole day to easing everyone's labour. In consequence of their decision, they suspended the use of their vocal chords for the day, and the bellow of their lungs was not heard at all. Paris was astonished not to hear the cry of the vendors, and the silence of this patriotic tocsin told the city, the faubourgs and the suburbs that the 1,200 chanticleers were hard at work on the field of Grenelle. . . . A young man arrives, takes off his coat, throws his two watches on top of it, takes a pickaxe and goes off to work some distance away. But your two watches? 'Oh! If one can't trust one's brothers. . . !' And this repository amongst the gravel and pebbles is as safe as in the safe-keeping of a deputy of the National Assembly.

The preparation of the great amphitheatre was finally completed—in time. According to a member of the American embassy staff, 'the spectacle of that day considered as a spectacle was really sublime and magnificent; the most perfect order and harmony reigned'. But there was a jarring note in some reports of the fête. One journal complained that, although the king happily put up with being soaked when he went hunting, he had not been prepared to venture out from his shelter to take an oath of loyalty to the nation. The Courrier de Provence *administered a ponderous rebuke to others who had betrayed the spirit of democracy:*

We would be failing in our duty if, having paid homage to the spirit of brotherhood which characterized this fête, to the spirit of liberty which was displayed in the procession, we were to pretend not to notice how this spirit changed on the field of the federation. . . . Admiration was not directed towards the people of Paris, who multiplied under our very feet, nor to the emblems of our liberty and its victories. It was fixed on the brilliant throne destined for the head of the government [Louis XVI]. The sight of this throne seemed to paralyse almost everybody, seemed to turn them to stone, so that, like the celebrated Circe, it transformed patriotic spirits into royalist ones. There was a vast upsurge of idolatry for the monarchy. People seemed to forget the restorers of French liberty—the National Assembly—and to see only one individual, he who formerly held in his hand all powers, powers which his ministers cruelly abused. . . . Was this becoming to a free people? Did they thus prove that they held a proper view of their own powers, or of the duties, of the existence of a king? Did it not prove that they have not yet thrown off the man of the past, that they still cling to their old ideas, their prejudices, their superstitious veneration of the monarchy?

Marat, that rabble-rouser whose violent language often cloaked a sound—though ruthless—common sense, did not mince words on the subject. All these fêtes and celebrations, he said in a pamphlet entitled C'en est fait de nous *('It's all up with us'), were merely intended to divert the people from the calamities which threatened them.*

Citizens of every age and every station! The measures taken by the National Assembly are not the kind to save you from destruction. It's all up with you, for always, if you do not run to arms, if you do not recapture that heroic valour which, on 14 July and 5 October, twice saved France. Fly to St-Cloud [the royal country residence] if there is still time. Bring back the king and the dauphin to within your walls, keep them under careful guard, and let them answer to you for what happens. Lock up the Austrian woman and her brother-in-law so that they may no longer conspire. Seize all the ministers and their henchmen, put them in irons. . . . Let the cannon be shared out among all the districts. . . . Hurry, hurry, if there is still time, or soon countless enemy legions will pounce upon you. Soon you will see the privileged orders rise again. Despotism, hideous despotism, will reappear, more formidable than ever.

Five or six hundred fallen heads would have ensured your peace, liberty, and happiness. A false humanity stayed your hands. It will cost the lives of millions of your brothers! Let your enemies triumph even for an instant and the blood will flow in torrents. They will slaughter you without pity. They will disembowel your wives. To extinguish among you for ever the love of liberty, their bloody hands will search the heart out from among the very entrails of your children.

But although Marat foresaw the holocaust that was to come, France in 1790 was comparatively peaceful. The National—or, more correctly, Constituent—Assembly was too concerned with the future to pay much attention to the present. The machinery of day-to-day government quietly subsided into chaos. The foundations of war between church and state were laid when a civil constitution was imposed on the clergy in July 1790 and denounced by the Vatican in March 1791. Trouble was brewing, but the harvest of 1789 had been a good one and full stomachs lent conviction to idealistic beliefs. William Wellesley-Pole, twenty-seven years old, and a British member of parliament, described Paris in September 1790 in these words:

The common people appear to me to be exactly as gay as I remember them . . . and notwithstanding they all talk the highest language in favour of the revolution, they laugh at the National Assembly without scruple, and say they had rather have aristocratical Louis then democratical *assignats*. . . .

Nothing can be more tiresome than all their new plays and operas; they are a heap of hackneyed public sentiments on general topics of the rights of men and duties of kings, just like Sheridan's grand paragraphs in the *Morning Post*. These are applauded to the skies. . . .

The aristocrats are melancholy and miserable to the last degree. This makes the society at Paris very gloomy; the number of deserted houses is immense, and if it were not for the deputies, ambassadors, and some refugees from Brussels, there would be scarcely a gentleman's coach to be seen in the streets.

The Flight to Varennes

The Vatican's rejection of the civil constitution of the church, which had the effect of turning the clergy into a branch of the civil service, was one of the events which at last stiffened the king's resolution to flee. For some time, the queen had been making preparations for just such a contingency. Late on the evening of 20 June 1791, the royal family and a few faithful retainers made their escape. The story is told by the Duchesse d'Angoulême, daughter of Louis XVI and Marie Antoinette, who was twelve years old at the time.

Throughout the day of 20 June 1791, my father and mother appeared to me to be very restless and preoccupied, for no reason I was aware of. After dinner, they sent us away, my brother and me, and shut themselves up alone with my aunt. I have since discovered that it was then that they told her of their projected flight. At five o'clock my mother went out for a walk with my brother and myself. . . .

During the walk, my mother took me aside, told me that I must not worry

10] Marie Antoinette and the royal children; the elder boy died in 1789

myself about what I would see, that we would never be separated for long, and that we would be together again very soon. My wits were dull, and I understood nothing of all this. She kissed me and told me that, if the attendants asked me why I was not myself, I must say that she had scolded me but that I had made it up with her again. We returned at seven o'clock; I went back to my apartments very drearily, understanding nothing at all of what my mother had said to me.

I was all alone. My mother had persuaded Madame de Mackau [the princess's governess] to go to the Visitation, where she went often, and had sent the young woman who usually attended me off to the country. I had scarcely lain down when my mother came in. She had instructed me to send away all my attendants on the pretext that I was indisposed, and only to keep one woman near me. When she came and found us alone, she told the woman and myself that we must leave immediately, and explained how it was to be arranged. She said to Madame Brunier—the woman who was with me—that she wished she might follow us, but that as she had a husband she could remain. This woman said immediately, without hesitation, that my mother was quite right to go; that she had been unhappy for too long and that, as for herself, she would instantly leave her husband and follow her wherever she wished. My mother was very affected by this mark of attachment.

My mother went back to her apartments and greeted Monsieur [the king's brother] and Madame, who had come as usual to sup with my father. Monsieur was aware of the projected journey; when he returned home, he went to bed, but rose again immediately and left with Monsieur d'Avaray, the young man who saved him from all perils on the road and who is with him still. As for Madame, she knew nothing; it was only when she had gone to bed that a Madame Gourbillon, who was her companion, came to tell her that she had been charged by the queen and Monsieur to see her out of France. Monsieur and Madame met again at a posting station, where they pretended not to know each other, and arrived safely at Brussels.

My brother had also been awakened by my mother, and Madame de Tourzel [his governess] led him to my mother's rooms downstairs. I went down with them. There we found one of the bodyguard, called Monsieur de Malden, who was to see us safely away. My mother came in to us several times. They dressed my brother as a little girl; he looked charming. As he was dropping with sleep, he did not know what was afoot. I asked him what he thought was going to happen, and he told me he believed we were to act a play, because we were in disguise. At half past ten, when we were quite ready, my mother herself led us to the coach, in the middle of the courtyard, which was a dangerous thing for her to do.

We entered the coach, Madame de Tourzel, my brother and I. Monsieur de Fersen [the Swedish admirer of Marie Antoinette, who made many of the escape preparations] was the coachman. Not to attract suspicion we took several turns round the city. Finally, we returned to the Petit Carrousel, which is very close to the Tuileries. My brother had settled down on the floor of the coach under Madame de Tourzel's skirts. We saw Monsieur de La Fayette pass—he had been to see the king ceremonially to bed—and we remained there waiting for a long hour, without knowing what was happening. Never has time appeared to me to pass more slowly. Madame de Tourzel was travelling under the name of the Baroness de Korff [a Russian lady then in Paris, in whose name a passport had been issued]. My mother was the governess of her children, and called herself Madame Rochet; my father was the valet-de-chambre, Durand; my aunt, a companion, Rosalie; my brother and myself the two daughters of Madame de Korff, with the names of Amélie and Aglaé. At last, after an hour, I saw a woman walking round the coach. I was afraid we had been discovered; but I was reassured when the coachman opened the carriage door and it was my aunt. She had escaped alone, with one of her attendants. Entering the coach, she trod on my brother who was on the floor, but he was brave enough not to cry out. She assured us that all was quiet and that my father and mother would be coming soon. In fact, my father arrived shortly after, and then my mother with the bodyguard who was to follow us. We took the road, and nothing happened until we reached the city gate. There, a travelling coach was to take us on. Monsieur de Fersen did not know where it was.

We had to wait there for a long time, and my father even got out, which caused us much concern. At last, Monsieur de Fersen returned, having found the other carriage. We changed coaches. Monsieur de Fersen wished my father good evening and rode off. The three bodyguards were Messieurs de Malden, Dumoutier, and Valory. The last acted as courier; the others as servants, one on horseback, the other seated outside the coach. They had changed their names. The first called himself Saint-Jean; the second Melchior; the other, François. The two femmes-de-chambre, who had left before us, rejoined us at Bondy [about eight miles from Paris]. They were in a small carriage. We set off. Day began to break. During the morning nothing happened worthy of note, but at six leagues from Paris we met with a man on horseback who kept following us. At Etoges, we thought we had been recognized. At four o'clock we passed the large town of Châlons-sur-Marne; there we were certainly recognized. Many people praised God to see the king, and offered prayers for the success of his flight.

At the posting station after Châlons, we were supposed to find mounted troops who would escort us as far as Montmédy; arrived there, we found no one. We remained in the expectation of meeting them until eight o'clock, then we went on in the last of the daylight to Clermont. There we did see some troops, but the entire village was in a ferment and refused to let them mount their horses. An officer recognized my father, approached him, and told him in a low voice that he was betrayed. We also saw Monsieur Charles de Damas there, but he could do nothing.

We continued on our way. Night had fallen and, in spite of our agitation and nervousness, everyone in the coach was asleep. We were awakened by a frightful jolt, and at the same time one of the men came to us to say that they did not know what had happened to the courier who had ridden ahead of the coach. Judge of our anxiety; we believed that he had been recognized and arrested. We were just outside the village of Varennes where there were scarcely a hundred houses and no posting station. Ordinarily, travellers send their own horses there in advance. We had done this, but they were at the château on the other side of the river, and no one knew where to find them. At last the courier reappeared . . . and someone came to say that the horses were at the château. The coachman started the coach moving again, but very quietly. Arrived in the village, we heard alarming shouts round the carriage. Stop! Stop! They seized the postilions and, in a moment, the carriage was surrounded with a mob of people, armed and carrying torches. They asked us who we were. We replied: 'Madame de Korff and her family.' They took some lights, held them up immediately in front of my father, and demanded that we should descend.

We said no, that we were simple travellers and that we must go on. They charged us to get out or they would kill us all; at the same instant, they all directed their muskets at the coach.

We descended and, crossing the street, we saw six mounted dragoons passing. Alas, they had no officer; otherwise, six determined men might well have been able to strike fear into everyone, and might have saved the king.

11] The royal family arrested at Varen

Had the king travelled in a less eye-catching conveyance; had he dispensed with his train of attendants; had he refrained from poking out of the carriage window a head known to all France from the very lifelike portrait printed on the new assignats; *had he taken any or all of these precautions, he might have saved himself. As it was, the royal family sat down to supper at Varennes, under the watchful eye of the inhabitants, until a body of patriot troops arrived. The next day they began their melancholy progress back to the capital.*

12] Under heavy guard, the royal family re-enters Paris

During his enforced residence at the Tuileries, Louis had given the impression of being stolidly, even benevolently, resigned to his fate. When he left for Varennes, however, he wrote a 'declaration to all Frenchmen' explaining his conduct. Nothing could have been better calculated to wreck his case. It consisted of a long catalogue of the insults to which he had been subjected, and made it clear that his apparent good humour had been only a mask. The National Assembly, he said, had arrogated to itself all his powers. He had been deprived of his beloved bodyguard. He had no effective veto on legislation. When he had come back from Versailles to the Tuileries in October 1789:

Nothing was ready to receive the king, and the arrangement of the apartments is very far from providing the conveniences to which His Majesty was accustomed in the other royal houses. . . . What remains to the king but an empty shadow of royalty? He has been allowed twenty-five millions for the expenses of his civil list; but the splendour of the house which he has to maintain to honour the dignity of the crown of France . . . must absorb the whole of that sum. . . .

Frenchmen! Is this what you expected when you sent representatives to the National Assembly? Did you want the anarchy and despotism of the clubs [i.e. political parties] to replace the monarchical government under which the nation has prospered for fourteen hundred years? Did you want to see your king outraged, deprived of his liberty, while he occupied himself only with establishing yours? A love for their kings is one of the virtues of the French, and His Majesty has personally received testimonies of it too touching for him ever to be able to forget them. The rebels well knew that, as long as this love persisted, their work would never be achieved.

The rebels, the king went on, had set about destroying this love by undermining the respect that was an integral part of it. Insult followed insult. Mr Necker was cheered more loudly than the king. A fanatic at the Palais Royal was applauded for suggesting that the queen should be shut up in a convent. At the fête of the federation in July 1790, the royal family had been seated apart from the king. 'The most insolent speeches, the most abominable suggestions echoed in His Majesty's ears.' There were other complaints in the same tenor. His Majesty concluded:

Frenchmen! And especially you, Parisians; you, inhabitants of a city which His Majesty's ancestors were pleased to call the good city of Paris! Beware the suggestions and the lies of your false friends; return to your king. He will always be your father, your best friend. What pleasure will he not take in forgetting all those personal affronts and seeing himself once more in your midst, when a constitution—which he will have accepted freely—will ensure that our holy religion is respected, that the government is established on a firm footing and that, through its actions, the property and condition of all the people will be no more subject to disturbance, the laws will be no more transgressed with impunity, and liberty will be placed on sure and stable foundations.

Lord Gower, the British ambassador in Paris, put the matter bluntly in his next despatch to the home government.

'If this country ceases to be a monarchy,' *he said*, 'it will be entirely the fault of Louis XVI. Blunder upon blunder, inconsequence upon inconsequence, a total want of energy of mind accompanied with personal cowardice, have been the destruction of his reign.'

Politics in 1791

Within three weeks of the king's return to Paris, republicanism had become a force to be reckoned with. Should the king continue to reign, or should France become a republic? Of all the newspapers, only the Révolutions de Paris *had enough foresight—or, perhaps, enough courage—to state the probable consequences of the ill-starred flight to Varennes.*

We have only one thing to say to the National Assembly. *We shall have war.*

We shall have it if Louis once more defiles the throne.

We shall have it if he is dethroned.

We shall have it if the law carries out vengeance on him.

We shall have it if we conserve the monarchy.

We shall have it if we establish a regency council.

We shall have it if we constitute ourselves a republic.

But in the first case the head of the army will be our most mortal enemy. In the second, this same enemy will still have a numerous following. In the third, his execution or permanent imprisonment will not purge France of the germ of tyranny; the little wolf-cub will be raised, at the expense of the state, to avenge the death of his father. In the fourth, we will be defeated, because a monarchy such as people hope to establish in France can sustain itself only through a contract of integrity between the representatives of the people and the head of the government, and integrity is incompatible with our royal prerogatives; a monarch could only be a cipher or a tyrant. In the fifth case, the regency council will have neither enough scope nor enough will, because it would act only subordinately; or, if it has scope, there will be everything to fear lest factions may arise. In the sixth and last case, we will win, because we will be free, clear of all fetters. . . .

It is time, it is more than time, to strike a great blow. Let the head of Louis fall . . . let the throne and all the high and mighty baubles of royalty be consigned to the flames. Let the National Assembly of monarchical days make way for a senate of the republic; let this address a manifesto to all the tyrants of Europe; let it invite all people to liberty; let it be the first campaign of immense legions of our new republicans to go and exterminate all despots, to plant the standard of liberty even in the very heart of Germany. We will be free then, we will anticipate the war that others are anxious to carry into our territory, and France will have the glory—unknown until that day—of having conquered, not Europe for France, but the universe for liberty, purging it of kings, emperors, and tyrants of all description.

It was all very well for a newspaper to indulge in such flights of fancy. The National Assembly had just spent the best part of two years drawing up a monarchical constitution, and had no desire to remove the monarch from the equation. The constitution was almost complete and needed the royal assent. In September, His Majesty attended a meeting of the assembly; the scene was reported by the Mercure de France:

An usher announced the king. The assembly rose. . . .

'Gentlemen, I have come here solemnly to consecrate the acceptance that I have given to the constitutional act. I therefore swear to be faithful to the nation and to the law; to employ all the power which is delegated to me to maintaining the constitution decreed by the National Constituent Assembly; and to see the laws carried out. May this great and memorable epoch see the re-establishment of peace, of unity, and become the pledge of the people's happiness and the prosperity of the empire.'

At the moment when the king pronounced the words: 'I swear to be faithful to the nation,' the assembly sat down. And Louis XVI for the first time in his life, the king of France for the first time since the foundation of the monarchy, swore—standing—allegiance to his seated subjects. They, become sovereign, saw no more in the king than their principal salaried official, legally subject to dismissal. After the words 'National Constituent Assembly', the king, becoming aware that he alone was standing, glanced round the room with a look in which benevolence gradually moderated to surprise, and His Majesty sat down and continued his speech.

The words 'National Constituent Assembly' have an authoritative ring about them. But was it a sober, dignified body on which France—and, indeed, the world—had fixed its eyes for the last two years? William Wellesley-Pole had described one of its sessions in the autumn of 1790:

They have no regular forms of debate on ordinary business. Some speak from their seats, some from the floor, some from the table, and some from the tribunes or desks. . . . They speak without preparation, and I thought many of them acquitted themselves well enough in that way, where only a few sentences were to be delivered. But on these occasions the riot is so great that it is very difficult to collect what is said. I am certain that I have seen above a hundred in the act of addressing the assembly together, all persisting to speak, and as many more replying in different parts of the House, sentence by sentence. Then the president claps his hands on both ears, and roars order, as if he was calling a coach. Sometimes he is quite driven to despair. He beats his table, his breast. . . . Wringing his hands is quite a common action, and I really believe he swears. . . . At last he seizes a favourable moment of quiet, either to put the question or to name who ought to speak. Then five hundred reclamations all at once renew the confusion, which seldom ends till the performers are completely hoarse, and obliged to give way to a fresh set.

The supercilious pen of the M.P. for East Looe traced a scene which was common-place for the next few years, but the tumult of the assembly's sittings did not mean that the deputies were failing to learn something of the technique of government. It was therefore all the more unfortunate that, when the Constituent Assembly's task was over, when it dissolved itself to make way for a new Legislative Assembly, it should have agreed to the grand renunciation proposed by Robespierre, ruling that no member of the outgoing Constituent Assembly should be eligible for election to the new Legislative Assembly.

With the new assembly, strong political personalities and groupings began to emerge. Some, like Brissot, were newly elected deputies; others, like Robespierre, were not eligible for re-election but were deeply involved in the Commune, *as the local govern-*

13] Brissot   14] Vergniaud   15] Condorcet

ment council of Paris was called. Throughout the revolution, the Commune *was willing and, often, able to arouse the people of Paris to demonstrations which had a powerful effect on the deliberations of the assembly.*

Those who were known as Brissotins, or Girondins (as some of them came from the Gironde), were held together by friendship, sentimental highmindedness, and a vague republicanism. J. F. Reichardt, a Prussian who visited France early in 1792, was not impressed by Brissot:

Brissot is small and common-looking. His yellow complexion, his eyes of the same hue, indicate a rather bilious temperament. He is the only one of the deputies I speak of in whose look I have not caught a glimpse of gaiety, or on whose lips an honest smile. So far, what I have heard him say has seemed to me flat and uninspired; one always feels a malevolent purpose in his speeches, which usually end in denunciations.

To Madame Roland, however, her friend Brissot became more estimable the better one knew him:

Brissot's simple manners, his frankness, his natural casualness, appeared to me to be in perfect harmony with the austerity of his principles. But I found in him a kind of instability of spirit and of character which did not so well suit the gravity of philosophy. It always pained me, and his enemies have made good use of it. . . . He is, however, the best of men, a good husband, loving father, faithful friend, virtuous citizen. His company is as pleasant as his temper is easy.

Madame Roland could not bring herself to like Vergniaud, the outstanding orator of the group, but Reichardt preferred him to Brissot:

Vergniaud, incontestably the most vigorous and serious of the popular orators, is quite another man! His face is disagreeable, but carries the imprint of strength and energy. His whole person gives the same impression, although he is neither tall nor distinguished. His gaze is hard and penetrating; he and Lacroix are the only orators [in the assembly] who have appeared to me to be motivated by sound convictions.

Of Condorcet, who was perhaps the most thoughtful of the Brissotins, Reichardt says:

Condorcet appears to have passed forty. He has a good presence; his aquiline nose, his well-shaped mouth, his pale complexion form a whole which is agreeable if a little lacking in distinction, but by no means vulgar. His expression, his words, his gestures disclose his vanity and self-satisfaction. This is, moreover, a trait which dominates all the deputies; the attitudes and the demeanour of five-sixths of the assembly indicate a conceit which sorts ill, in my opinion, with the task of legislation.

Madame Roland herself was the wife of, and the power behind, one of the king's new Brissotin ministers. She was charming, intelligent, efficient, attractive, and more than a little sanctimonious. One of her dearest friends, Sophie Grandchamp, recalled her first meeting with Marie-Jeanne-Phlipon—sometimes called Manon—Roland.

I have difficulty in describing the impression I received. I can still see that celebrated woman, seated near a little table, in Amazonian costume, her black hair cut in jockey style, her expression animated, her eyes sweet yet piercing. . . . Seated near her, I paid little attention to what was going on; I thought only of looking at her, of listening to her. She expressed herself with a purity, a use of language, a vivacity which the silvery timbre of her voice rendered even more remarkable.

These were the Girondins. They were comparatively moderate in their political opinions, and very often dishonest in their tactics. Their opponents, the Jacobins, were

16] Madame Roland   17] Robespierre   18] Danton

more extreme, more honest, more efficient, and much more ruthless. Early in 1791, a British political writer who lived in France, William Augustus Miles, summed up his impressions of Robespierre:

He is cool, measured and resolved. He is *in his heart* republican, honestly so, not to pay court to the multitude but from an opinion that it is the very best, if not the only, form of government which men ought to admit. . . . He is a stern man, rigid in his principles, plain, unaffected in his manners, no foppery in his dress, certainly above corruption, despising wealth, and with nothing of the volatility of a Frenchman in his character. . . . I watch him very closely every night. I read his countenance with eyes steadily fixed on him. He is really a character to be contemplated; he is growing every hour into consequence and, strange to relate, the whole National Assembly hold him cheap, consider him as insignificant, and, when I mentioned to one of them my suspicions and said he would be the man of sway in a short time and govern the million, I was laughed at.

Madame Roland, looking back in 1793 from a prison cell at the man who had once attended political gatherings in her house, was understandably sour:

Robespierre spoke little, sniggered often, tossed off a few pieces of sarcasm, never disclosed an opinion. . . . Never did the smile of confidence rest on his lips, though they were often contracted in the bitter laugh of an envy which tried to pass for disdain.

Danton could hardly have been expected to appeal to Madame Roland's delicate sensibilities:

I looked at this repulsive, odious face and, although I told myself that one should not judge anyone on hearsay, that I knew nothing definite against him, that even the most honest man must have two reputations in times of dissension, that finally one should distrust appearances, I could not reconcile the idea of a good man with that face. I have never seen anything which so perfectly characterized the violence of brutal passions, the most astounding audacity, but half veiled by an air of great joviality, an affectation of frankness and a kind of good nature.

Of Saint-Just, that cold, rigid, and frightening young man who came to regard himself as the avenging angel of the revolution, the journalist Camille Desmoulins said:

The member of the Convention who has the highest opinion of himself is Saint-Just. One can see by his attitude and bearing that he looks upon his

19] Saint-Just   20] Marat

own head as the corner-stone of the revolution, for he carries it upon his shoulders with as much respect as if it were the Sacred Host.

Marat is the last in the present gallery of revolutionary personalities. He christened himself 'the friend of the people' and called his journal by the same name. His vitriolic pen and cantankerous personality endeared him to no one; he could not be controlled even by his Jacobin friends. L.-S. Mercier, a Girondin deputy who was also a successful author, later poured down vituperation on the memory of Marat, who, he said:

. . . united meanness of face and figure with that of character and mind, whose insolence at the rostrum was a matter for ridicule, who was superior only to his valets, who will nevertheless occupy more than one page of history. History will at least say that if this vile demagogue . . . drove a blind multitude on to pillage and crime, he did not dare to preach atheism.

That, concluded Mercier, was to be left to others among the abominable Jacobins.

21 and 22] A *sans-culotte* and his wife

The Revolution goes to War

The Girondins wanted power, but to win this they needed popular support. France was at this time in the state of uneasy lethargy which so often forms the anti-climax of great events, and there seemed nothing in domestic politics likely to restore the impassioned unity of the early days of the revolution. In August 1791, however, Marie Antoinette's brother—the Emperor Leopold—and Frederick William of Prussia had been considerate enough to issue the Declaration of Pilnitz:

His Majesty the Emperor and His Majesty the King of Prussia, having listened to the wishes and representations of Monsieur and of Monsieur le Comte d'Artois [Louis XVI's brothers], jointly declare that they regard the situation in which the King of France finds himself at this time as a matter of interest common to all the Sovereigns of Europe. They trust that this interest cannot fail to be recognized by the Powers whose aid they claim, and that in consequence these Powers will not refuse to employ, conjointly with Their said Majesties, the most efficacious means, proportionate to their forces, to put the King of France in a position to strengthen, in the most perfect freedom, the foundations of a monarchical government equally consonant with the rights of the Sovereigns and the well-being of the French Nation. Then, and in this event, Their said Majesties the Emperor and the King of Prussia are resolved to act promptly, with mutual accord, with the forces necessary to achieve the proposed and common end. In the meantime, they will order their troops to hold themselves ready for action.

This ingenious document implied that all the powers of Europe were preparing themselves to go to war with France, and this was how it was read by the French. In fact, the Emperor Leopold was hedging his bets; if everyone else agreed to go to war, he would do so too, with the glory of having organized a grand alliance; if everyone else would not *go to war, the blame could hardly be laid at his door. The state of Europe at the time was, in fact, such that everyone was anxious to avoid conflict.*

But, to the Girondins, war offered the best of all ways of uniting the French people behind them. Robespierre, foreseeing its effect on domestic politics and fearing, too, its ill effects on the whole progress of the revolution, was almost alone in trying to stem the rising tide. In the early months of 1792, he made a series of long and brilliant speeches in the Jacobin club, but even there war-like sentiment ran too strong.

This is, perhaps, the place to say more about the Jacobin club. It had begun in the early days of the States-General, when a handful of deputies from Brittany (later joined by deputies from other areas) took to meeting in a café to discuss policy. When the assembly moved to Paris, the 'Breton club' hired a hall in the Jacobin convent in the rue St-Honoré and soon came to be known as the Jacobin club. Its prestige was enormous, and the other political clubs that sprang up all over France began to look to it for leadership. Ultimately, the Jacobin club of Paris became almost an auxiliary of the government as well as the centre of its propaganda. That indefatigable sightseer, J. F. Reichardt, attended a meeting of the club in March 1792:

The president, the proctors, the speaker at the rostrum, many of the club members and the people in the public galleries wore the red bonnet. It is decidedly an odious head-dress! . . . All the speakers who mounted the rostrum had it on their heads. One deputy from Lyon appeared without the bonnet and a member threw him his; the deputy at first took the thing as a joke and sent the object back to its owner; but a second bonnet was thrown, the tribunes began to shout 'the bonnet! the bonnet!' and he had to put one on. As these head-dresses are without doubt going to play an important role, I will send you a specimen. . . .

Robespierre showed himself at this session, but did not say a word. He struck me by his insolence. Coming in, after having flung himself with a supercilious air into an isolated chair near the door, he remained motionless, tilting his well-curled head backwards. He did not take the least part in the debates and seemed to be there only because he makes use of club members and because he wanted to see if some incident might take place which could prove of interest to him. His flat, almost squashed-looking face, his pale complexion, his sly look, made the insolence of his attitude even more provoking.

After the minutes of the previous session had been read, there appeared a deputation of twenty soldiers led by an under-officer who declaimed, in tragic accents, a speech asking for the assistance of the Jacobins in supporting a proposition which he intended to submit the next day to the assembly.

A deputation from the municipality of Lyon succeeded him and formulated a similar request.

A National Guardsman, who had been on duty at the château in the morning, then mounted the rostrum to speak animatedly about a conflict on precedence which had arisen between the king's guard and the National Guard. . . .

Someone read an interminable report on the troubles at Arles where, as in many other towns of the Midi, there are threats of counter-revolution. . . . After having wearied us for an hour, the speaker at last said something worth while. He submitted that as the result of an aberration for which the ministers and the aristocrats were responsible, the nation had been divided into two inimical parts—patriots, and counter-revolutionaries or aristocrats. This error was the point of departure for the civil dissensions which are breaking out at all points. The *entire* nation accepted the constitution through the medium of its representatives; so there only remain rebels who try to deny the unanimity of the nation and argue the constitution from abroad. But inside France, there *can* exist parties discussing these questions from diverse viewpoints and seeking to make their own opinion prevail by means of persuasion or force; the nation, which has accepted the constitution, ought not to interfere between these adversaries.

There is much truth in these assertions. The speaker did not know how to develop them—and I did not have the right to do so!

Austria was an hereditary enemy of France. That fact, and the threats in the Declaration of Pilnitz, and the Girondins' intensive campaign in favour of a 'war of peoples against kings', all had their effect. On 20 April 1792, Louis XVI—hoping that the French armies would be defeated and that he would regain his throne as a result —declared war on Austria. France's armies were in a deplorable state, the food situation was bad, the economy was unstable, the king's ministers had no idea of how a war should be conducted. It was hardly surprising that the first few months of hostilities were almost catastrophic.

Robespierre, unable to avert the war, turned his attention towards making it successful. In the first issue of his journal, the Défenseur de la Constitution, *he said:*

The war . . . has opened with a reverse; it must finish with the triumph of liberty, or the last Frenchman must have disappeared into the earth. But to carry out this grand design, there must be other methods than the little tricks of intrigue and the empty declamations of political charlatans. There must be all the wisdom and all the energy of a free people. There must even be a tracing back to the true causes of our errors and our reverses, so that we may atone for them by exploits worthy of our cause. . . .

To make war profitably against the enemy without, it is a standard measure,

23] The declaration of war announced in the Jacobin cl

24] The volunteers go off to war

absolutely indispensable, to make war against the enemies within—that is to say, against injustice, against aristocracy, against treachery, against tyranny. If this system is followed faithfully, you will be able to regard war as a benefit. But if you see reigning inside France a military despotism and a cruel tyranny, disguised under the veil of the law and the semblances of public safety, if you see growing each day discord and oppression, if men's contempt, forgetfulness of the declaration of rights, the sway of Machiavellism, of intrigue and of corruption replace the regenerative principles on which liberty rests, you must believe that you have been deceived by those perfidious counsellors who have drawn you such dazzling pictures. . . .

Frenchmen, fight and stay on watch at all times; watch during your defeats, watch during your victories; distrust your tendency towards enthusiasm, and put yourselves on guard even against the glory of your generals. . . . Watch lest there arise in France a citizen so redoubtable that he one day becomes the master, who will deliver you to the court and reign in its name, or wipe out both people and monarch to raise, on their common ruins, a legal tyranny, the worst of all despotisms.

Had Robespierre been gifted with second sight, he could hardly have foretold more accurately the pattern of events in France for the next twenty years.

The End of the Monarchy

On 25 July, the enemy general, the Duke of Brunswick, issued a manifesto threatening that, if any harm were done to the royal family, Paris itself would pay the ultimate penalty. Revolutionary ardour did not seem to be cutting much ice on the battlefields. There was unrest in the provinces. Various staple foodstuffs were in short supply. The Paris Commune *had become more revolutionary than ever. Marat, in his* Ami du Peuple, *and Hébert, in the less stylish but more obscene* Père Duchesne, *poured out a torrent of denunciation against the royalist and moderate parties. By 9 August 1792, the crisis had come. Madame de Tourzel, governess to the royal children, tells the story of what it felt like to be the target of the rancour of a whole city:*

Monsieur de Paroy, fearing for the lives of their Majesties and Monseigneur le Dauphin, begged me to offer the queen three cuirasses of twelve folds of taffetas, impenetrable by bullet or dagger, which he had had made for her, the king, and Monseigneur le Dauphin. He sent me a dagger wherewith to try them. I took them to the queen, who at once tried on that intended for her and, seeing me with the dagger in my hand, said to me with the utmost coolness: 'Strike me, and see if it answers.' I could not endure such an idea; it made me shudder, and I said that nothing would induce me to do such a thing. She then took off her cuirass and I seized it; I put it on over my dress and struck it with the dagger, and, as Monsieur de Paroy had said, I found it impenetrable. The queen then agreed with the king that they should each of them put one on at the slightest symptom of danger, and they did so. This incident will give an idea of the horrible position of the royal family, and the occupants of the Tuileries who were reduced to the employment of such devices.

Great care was taken by the rebels to foster the excitement which prevailed among the inhabitants of the faubourgs, the provincial troops and those from Marseilles. Drink and money were given to them; and, emboldened by the rebel leaders who called them together and incited them to bloodshed, they conceived the most frightful projects. . . .

The king, alive at last to the necessity of defending himself in case of attack, sent for ninety Swiss from Courbevoie for the defence of the château. . . . Whole bodies of the National Guard had ranged themselves on the side of the rebels, so that the king had only the Swiss to rely upon, together with six hundred men of the National Guard and about three hundred others, gentlemen, officers of the Royal Guard, and servants of His Majesty, armed only with swords and pistols, all sincerely attached to him, and dressed in civilian attire so as not to give any umbrage to the National Guard.

In the council chamber, before the door of the king's room, there were about twenty grenadiers of the National Guard, to whom the queen addressed these words: 'Gentlemen, all that you hold dear, your wives and children, depend on our existence; our interests are one.' And pointing to the little knot of gentlemen who were in the rooms, she added: 'You cannot distrust these brave men, who will share your danger, and will defend you to their last breath.' Moved to tears, they swore to die, if necessary, in defence of their Majesties.

Nobody in the château went to bed; everybody remained in the apartments, anxiously awaiting the outcome of a day which broke under such sinister auspices. The queen spoke to everybody in the most kindly manner, and gave heart to all. I and my daughter Pauline spent the night by the side of Monseigneur le Dauphin, whose calm and peaceful slumbers were in striking contrast with the agitation that reigned in every mind.

About 4 a.m. [on the 10th] I went to the apartments of the king to find out what was going on, and what we had to hope or fear. 'Today', said Monsieur d'Hervilly to me, 'I anticipate the worst; the worst thing to do is to do nothing and, as a matter of fact, nothing *is* being done.'

About 7 a.m. it was announced that the inhabitants of the faubourgs and the Marseillais were advancing against the château. . . .

The king, who had already sent to the assembly to request that a deputation might be dispatched to overawe the rebels, renewed his request through Monsieur Dejoly, minister of justice; but under the pretext that a sufficient number of members were not present, Cambon succeeded in carrying the adjournment of the house, despite the perilous position of the king, which grew worse at every moment.

The uncertainty in regard to what step to take in such imminent danger appeared to Roederer [an official of the assembly] to be a favourable opportunity for inducing the king to proceed to the assembly. He went to His Majesty . . . and, begging him to send away the large number of persons about him, spoke to him as follows: 'Sire, the danger is imminent; the authorities have no force at their disposal and defence is impossible. Your Majesty and your family, as well as everybody in the château, are in the greatest danger; to prevent bloodshed there is no other resource than to repair to the assembly.' The queen, who was standing by the king, remarked that it was impossible to abandon all the brave men who had come to the château solely to defend the king. 'If you oppose this step,' said Roederer to her in a severe tone of voice, 'you will be responsible, Madame, for the lives of the king and your children.' The poor unhappy queen was silent and experienced such a revulsion of feeling that her face and neck became suffused with colour. She was distressed beyond measure to see the king listen to the advice of a man so justifiably suspect, and she appeared to foresee all the misfortunes that awaited her. Roederer held out great hopes to the royal family of the success of this proceeding and of their speedy return to the château. The queen, though far from believing him, repeated his words to those whom she was so grieved to leave. The king, deeply moved, turned to this faithful band and could only say to them: 'Gentlemen, I beg of you to withdraw and abandon a useless defence; there is nothing more to be done here either for you or for me.'

There was general consternation when the king was seen leaving for the assembly. The queen accompanied him, holding her two children by the hand. By their side were Madame Elisabeth and the Princesse de Lamballe, who, as a relative of their Majesties, was permitted to accompany them. I walked behind Monseigneur le Dauphin. The king was accompanied by his ministers and escorted by a detachment of the National Guard. . . .

At the door to the assembly there was a crowd who made us fear momentarily for the lives of the king and queen. A passage was at length made for them, and they were received by a deputation sent by the assembly for that purpose. The king crossed the hall accompanied by his ministers and placed himself by the side of the president. The queen, with her children and suite, stood opposite. 'I am come, gentlemen', said the king, 'to avoid a serious attack, believing that I cannot be in greater security than in your midst.' Vergniaud, who was presiding, replied: 'You may rely, Sire, on the firmness of the assembly; its members have sworn to die in order to maintain the rights of the constituted authorities.'

The king then took his seat by the side of the president, and the royal family sat on the ministerial bench. But as several members of the assembly pointed out that deliberation in the presence of the king was forbidden by the constitution, the assembly decided that the king and the royal family should withdraw to the reporters' gallery behind the presidential chair. The faithful servants of His Majesty at once tore down the barriers of this gallery and, for a portion of the day, were thus in communication with the royal family.

Roederer appeared at the bar to give an account of what was going on in Paris. . . . 'We have this moment heard that the château has been broken into.'

The assembly passed a decree placing persons and property under the safeguard of the people, and sent a deputation of twenty-five of its members to convey this declaration. Scarcely had it set out than the noise of cannon and musketry was heard. The deputation dispersed, and some members of it returned to the hall. The king reassured them by telling them that he had given orders that there was to be no firing; but the assembly, seeing armed men trying to enter the room, stopped them. Even in the midst of its success, the assembly was half dead with fear, always dreading lest somebody should appear on the scene to deliver the king and lay violent hands on the rebels.

Some petitioners arrived who said that the Swiss had lured them on by friendly signals and had shot a large number of them. 'We have set fire to the Tuileries,' they said, 'and we will not put it out until the people have obtained justice to their satisfaction. We are charged once more to demand the removal from office of the head of the government; we demand and expect this justice from you.' The president replied: 'The assembly is watching over the safety of the empire; assure the people that it is about to consider the important measures its safety demands.'

A deputation from the Thermes section appeared at the bar to state that it agreed with the petition . . . that the people, wearied of the crimes of the court, had sworn to maintain liberty and equality, and that every citizen in Paris shared these sentiments. 'Dare you swear', they said to the deputies, 'that you will save the empire?' 'Yes,' replied the deputies, rising to their feet, 'we swear it.'

The concert of all these seditious voices, joined with the noise of cannon

Attack on the Tuileries, 10 August 1792

and musketry, made us all fearful. Each discharge of cannon made us tremble; the king and queen were in extreme distress; and we were plunged in profound sorrow as we thought of the fate that was perhaps at that very moment befalling those we had left in the Tuileries. The poor little dauphin cried, thought of those whom he loved and had left behind in the château, threw himself in my arms, and kissed me. . . .

26] The crowd invades the assembly; the royal family is in the reporters' box

Several faithful servants of the king, having found means of access to the assembly, went to the king in the reporters' gallery and gave His Majesty an account of what was going on at the Tuileries. . . . These gentlemen told us that the Swiss had got the upper hand for a moment, but, as they were unsupported and the crowd increased every moment, they had been compelled to retire; that a great number of them were killed, and that the general fury had extended to the attendants of private individuals, of whom several, and especially mine, had perished; and that it was impossible to help feeling that there would be many more victims, so great was the rage which animated the mob, who were by this time masters of the château.

At this moment news was brought that the Swiss were marching against the assembly, that the provincial troops were on their way to meet them, and that a bloody engagement was about to take place. The assembly was afraid, and requested the king to permit one of those around him to go and parley with them and make them give up their arms. The president proposed that the order should be given in writing and Monsieur d'Hervilly offered to undertake the commission; but before starting he declared that he could not act to any purpose unless he had the order and signature of His Majesty. The assembly, afraid of the possible arrival of the Swiss, hastened to give the king pen, ink, and paper, so that he might give the order for them to lay down their arms and withdraw. Monsieur d'Hervilly crossed the rue St-Honoré amid a shower of bullets which rained on him from all sides, and he was admired by all these maniacs for his bravery. Seeing with sorrow how impossible it was for the Swiss to resist the multitude of armed men who were hurrying to meet them, he conveyed to them the king's order that they were to lay down their arms, and he returned to report the result of his commission.

The Marseillais and other brigands, seeing the Swiss disarmed, rushed upon them and the latter were obliged to hide themselves and change their clothes in order to avoid falling victims to the popular fury.

The king's departure from the Tuileries, however sensible it seemed at the time, appeared like callous desertion of those who had been faithful to him. If he had remained, he might have stopped the Swiss from firing and prevented the slaughter that followed. As it was, the people ran wild. Even Thomas Blaikie, convinced royalist that he was, was critical:

I could see the people running to and fro in the Champs Elizee, and the horror of the misacre increased as the king left his guards and went to the Nationale Assembly, so that those poor wretches that had come to defend him, being deserted by him, was now left to be misacred by the rabble. Whereas if the king had stopt, there was the greatest part of the Sections was ready to defend him. But when they found he had gone to the assembly they all turned to the mesacre of the poor Suiss gardes which could find no place of refuge as the barriers [city gates] was shut. . . . Many of these anthrophages passed in the street and stopt to show us parts of the Suisses they had misacred—some of whom I knew, and certainly before that would not have thought of any such thing. However, the example seemed a rage, and everyone seemed to glory in what he had done and to show even their furrie upon the dead body by cutting them or even tearing their clothes as monuments of triumph, so that this seemed as if the people were struck with madness.

The Legislative Assembly suspended the king from his functions. The monarchical constitution thus became inoperative and a new assembly had to be summoned. Instructions were issued for the election of a National Convention which was to guide France—if that is the word—through the next crucial years. This time there was no self-denying ordinance against re-election and the new Convention numbered among its members Brissot and most of the Girondins as well as Robespierre, Danton, and many leading Jacobins. The belligerents in the political war which was to bring so much bloodshed to France were girding themselves for battle.

The September Massacres

Before the new Convention could be elected, however, there was to take place one of the least justifiable events of the whole revolution. The king and his family were immured in the Temple, but political ferment had not died. The assembly yielded to public demand that those who had taken part in the 'royalist plot'—which everyone believed had been foiled by the action of the people on 10 August—should be punished. On 21 August, the guillotine was first used to behead a political prisoner. On 28 August, Danton, now minister of the interior under Roland, was granted the power to comb Paris for 'enemies of the revolution'. When news came on 2 September of the enemy attack on Verdun, the Commune *issued a panicky call 'To arms! The enemy is at our gates!'*

Paris was struck with a nameless terror. Whether the events of the next few days were controlled by ruthless politicians has never been proved; on the whole, it seems unlikely. But whoever started them, no one made any determined attempt to stop them. Something like thirteen hundred prisoners were massacred after the merest sketch of a trial. Many were refractory priests, some were aristocrats, a few were merely detained 'on suspicion'; the majority of those who died were, however, the ordinary tenants of eighteenth-century prisons, the thieves, the bullies, the prostitutes, the murderers of a capital city. If there is a rational explanation of the hysterical blood-letting that took place between 2 and 6 September, it is the one advanced at the time. The citizens were being called to arms; they suspected that when they left Paris, all the blackguards behind bars would break out and murder the women and children left behind. 'Justice' must be exercised first, then the men of Paris could set off to save their country with an easy mind.

Hearing of what was taking place at the prisons, that strange recorder of the Parisian scene, Restif de la Bretonne, went out to investigate:

We went up to the door of the prison [the Abbaye] without hindrance. A group of onlookers was there in a circle; the killers were at the door, inside as well as out. The judges were in the jailer's office.

Someone took the prisoners in to them. Someone asked their names. Someone traced them in the jail register. What they were accused of decided their fate. An eye-witness told me that often the killers inside pronounced sentence at the same time as the judges. A big man with a cold, grave air was taken to them. He was accused of ill-will and of aristocratic sympathies. He was asked if he was guilty. 'No, I have done nothing; it was only that they were suspicious about my beliefs, but in the three months I have been in prison no one has found anything against me.' These words made the judges incline towards leniency, but a man with a Provençal accent shouted: 'An aristocrat! To the Force [prison]! To the Force!'

'To the Force, let it be,' replied the man. 'I will not be any the more guilty for changing prisons.' He was not aware, that unfortunate soul, that the expression 'To the Force', spoken at the Abbaye, was sentence of death; just as the cry 'To the Abbaye', uttered in the other prisons, meant dispatch to the slaughter-house. He was propelled outside by the man who had shouted, over the threshold of death. At the first sabre stroke, he stood astonished;

27] The massacre at the women's prison of the Salpétrière on 3 September

but then he lowered both hands and let himself be killed without making a move.

I, who have never been able to bear seeing blood flow, judge how I felt finding myself jostled almost under the sabres. I trembled! I felt myself weakening and I threw myself to one side. A piercing cry from a prisoner less Spartan in the face of death than the others aroused in me a salutary indignation which restored me legs to take myself off with. I did not see any more. . . .

Next day, 3 September, the queen's foster-brother and valet-de-chambre, Weber, found himself in imminent danger. He did not realize this at the time, for he was a prisoner in the Force prison and no one was quite sure what was going on outside, even when armed men erupted into the cells:

They entered like furies, took us by the lapels, shook us vigorously, calling us scoundrels and aristocrats and accusing us of trying to hide ourselves. They added, with a thousand blasphemies, that they would never let us go and that they intended to get the whole truth out of us. As I did not then know that we were probably being marched off to our deaths, I gave way to all the indignation that this treatment inspired in me. I grasped one of these men who were armed to the teeth, I took another by the lapel and, shaking them in my turn in the most energetic fashion, I said to them: 'The turnkey must have told you that we are neither rascals nor people who would hide themselves; you ought to respect misfortune, if you have any feeling, and especially remember that the law forbids maltreating prisoners without knowing if they are guilty.'

Stunned by my boldness, they looked at each other for a moment and let me go. I went on: 'An honest man does not resist when it is a matter of obeying the law; but you are only despicable bullies; you are armed and I am not. Your conduct tells me you are cowards. Like you, I serve in the National Guard; like you, I can lay down arms one moment and take them up the next. I invite you to attack me then.'

The turnkeys having spoken to them in our favour, these minions began to treat us with a little more respect; they nevertheless ordered us to follow them, because it was, they said, their duty to take us before the tribunal established in the jailer's office.

When we left the inner courtyard, escorted by two armed men, I lost sight of my companions in misfortune, and being unable to guess what was signified by the number of naked and bloodstained sabres I could see, and the cries 'To the Abbaye, to the Abbaye' with which a prisoner was from time to time accompanied to the street door, I awaited my turn with resignation at the door to the room in which the hearings were being held.

It was ten o'clock in the morning when I was taken in. I saw a man, very corpulent, in the uniform of the National Guard and draped with a tricolour scarf, seated near a big table on which were placed the prison registers; beside the man with the scarf, who was carrying out the duties of president of the people's tribunal, was seated the prison clerk and round the table there were two grenadiers, two fusiliers, two foot-soldiers, and two market porters. These were the persons who composed the tribunal; finally, a mob of men from Marseilles and other provincial troops filled the room as spectators.

The president began my interrogation thus: 'Name, age, place of birth?' He then set himself to searching in the register for the item concerning me, which was called, in prison parlance, the screw. The prison clerk pointed it out to him with his finger; it appeared to me to consist of about twenty lines.

After having glanced over it and found that I was held for four crimes of *lèse-nation* [high treason against the nation], and especially for having passed the night of 10 August at the château [Tuileries], he restricted himself (and even today I still do not know why) to asking me this question: 'Why were you, on 9 and 10 August, at the Tuileries?' I replied: 'I served in the National Guard at Versailles, but for some time, my affairs having prevented me from doing my service, I paid exactly forty sous every day to a citizen who took my place. The National Assembly having afterwards decreed that every man with his own house should be regarded as of independent means and therefore obliged to do his own guard duty in future, I entered my name in the section where I live and carried out my service there punctually.' I went on: 'In the last three months I have done guard duty twice at the National Assembly and as many times at the château. Having received on the 9th at seven o'clock in the morning an instruction from Monsieur Tassin (the commander of the battalion) to report immediately at the guard-house, I was sent as reinforcement with nineteen of my comrades to the courtyards of the château under the command of Messieurs Guicher (lieutenant) and Laurent (sub-lieutenant) and I remained there by the order of my commanders until the last moment.'

The president, having listened to me with close attention, addressed the following words to those present: 'Does any of you, citizens, have knowledge of the facts that citizen Weber has just given to justify himself?' Several persons rose to attest that they were perfectly informed of all that I had just asserted, and that I had said nothing but what was in line with the truth. A small foot-soldier, especially, confirmed by word and gesture the accuracy of all my replies.

'Then I no longer see', said the president rising from his seat and taking off his hat, 'the least difficulty in proclaiming monsieur's innocence.' And he began to shout, with all the spectators, 'Vive la nation!' He ordered me to do the same; I obeyed, and I shouted with them, 'Vive la nation!' This second ceremony ended, the president proclaimed my innocence in these terms: 'You are free, citizen, but the country is in danger; you must enrol and leave for the frontier within three days.'

As, after his earlier pronouncement, I thought myself entirely out of danger, I replied: 'It is absolutely impossible, citizen president, for me to conform with that last order; I have an elderly, invalid mother and an unfortunate sister; they both need my help, they have only me to lean on, and I must return to them; I cannot abandon them.'

Two men behind me responded suddenly, in suppressed fury: 'Citizen, this is not the time to give reasons like that; everyone must go to war; the country needs soldiers; we ourselves, as good patriots, have forgotten that we are husbands and fathers; forget, as we have done, that you have a mother and a sister.'

The president, after having thrown a glance at the prison clerk as if to say that it would be his fault if I perished, gazed at me closely and said rather peevishly: 'I warn you, monsieur, that you must enrol. You must leave for the frontier without delay; I see nothing else for you.' He paused.

His looks, his gestures, and the tone of his voice having made me suspect some mystery, I made up my mind immediately, and, in the hope of getting away from them soon (for I would rather have died than take arms against my sovereign or against the interests of my benefactors), I replied with pretended serenity: 'Since you have need of me, monsieur, I will go to the frontiers whenever you please.'

This reply roused once more throughout the room cries of 'Vive la nation!' The president hastened to fill up my enrolment and made me sign the draft and my identity card.

Although Weber's trials were by no means over, since his royalist associations were discovered shortly after his 'release', he did escape with his life. Many other prisoners at the Force as well as at Bicêtre, Salpétrière, and elsewhere, were less fortunate. Restif de la Bretonne ventured out again on the second day of the massacres:

I go out. I listen, I follow groups of people hurrying to see the 'disasters'— for that is their word. Passing the Conciergerie, I see a killer who, someone tells me, is a sailor from Marseilles. His wrist is swollen with fatigue. I go on my way. The front of the Châtelet is ornamented with piled-up dead. I turn to run.

But instead I followed the people. I arrived [at the Force] in the rue St-Antoine, at the end of the rue des Ballets, just at the moment when one poor wretch, having seen them kill his predecessor, instead of stopping when

28] The head of the Princesse de Lamballe, friend of Marie Antoinette,
paraded round the Temple

he came through the gate took to his heels and ran for it. A man who was not one of the killers, but just one of those unthinking machines of whom there are so many, stopped him with his pike. The miserable fugitive was overtaken by his pursuers and murdered. The pikeman said to us dispassionately: 'Well, how was I to know they wanted to kill him. . . ?'

There had been a pause in the murders. Something was going on inside . . . I deluded myself that all was over. At last, I saw a woman appear, as white as a sheet, supported by a turnkey. They said to her harshly: 'Cry: "Vive la nation!"' 'No! No!' said she. They made her climb on a heap of corpses. One of the killers grabbed the turnkey and pushed him away. 'Ah!' exclaimed the ill-fated woman, 'do not harm him!' They repeated that she must shout 'Vive la nation!' She refused, disdainfully. Then one killer seized her, tore away her dress, and ripped open her stomach. She fell, and was finished off by the others. Never has my imagination envisaged such horror. I wanted to flee; my legs gave way under me. I fainted.

When I returned to my senses, I saw the bloody head. Someone told me they were going to wash it, curl it, stick it on the end of a pike, and carry it past the windows of the Temple. What pointless cruelty! . . .

This ill-fated woman was Madame de Lamballe.

The number of active killers who took part in the September massacres was only about one hundred and fifty. The rest of Paris looked on in fear or approval, or stayed behind closed shutters.

In the Temple

Within a fortnight of Paris's darkest days, the situation changed radically. The soldiers of the revolution won a dazzling victory in the battle zone and the forces of the Duke of Brunswick—who had threatened the city with fire and slaughter—went into ignominious retreat.

Among the comparatively few foreigners who still remained in Paris was Dr John Moore, father of the famous English general:

The public walks are crowded with men, women, and children of all conditions, with the most gay, unconcerned countenances imaginable. A stranger just come to Paris, without having heard of the late transactions, and walking through the gardens of the Tuileries, Place de Louis XVI, and Champs Élysées, would naturally imagine from the frisky behaviour and

29] The public promenade at the Palais Royal in 1792

cheerful faces of the company he meets that this day was a continuation of a series of days appointed for dissipation, mirth, and enjoyment. He could not possibly imagine that the ground he is walking over was so largely covered with the bodies of slaughtered men; or that the gay lively people he saw were so lately overwhelmed with sorrow and dismay.

I drove to many places in Paris this morning. The epithet 'royal', which was formerly so profusely assumed and inscribed with pride and ostentation, is now carefully effaced from every shop, magazine, auberge, or hotel; all those who were so vain of announcing over their doors that they were the tradesmen of the king or queen, or in any way employed by them, have removed every word, emblem, or sign which could revive the remembrance of such a connection. And at present a tailor would rather advertise that he was breeches-maker to a *sans-culottes* than to a prince of the blood royal.

The royal family was shut up in the Temple where, although they were strictly guarded, they did not at first suffer too great privation. A report on their diet was made to the Commune *in October:*

Louis XVI and his family have in the Temple twelve domestics engaged in the kitchens: a head cook, a plain cook, an assistant cook, a scullion, a turnspit, a steward and assistant, a boy, a keeper of the plate, and three waiters.

Breakfast. In the morning the steward provides for breakfast seven cups of coffee, six of chocolate, a pot of thick cream, a decanter of cold syrup, another of barley-water, three rounds of butter, a plate of fruit, six rolls, three loaves, a bowl of powdered sugar, a bowl of lump sugar, a salt-cellar.

Not all of this is consumed by the prisoners. The remnants are made use of by the three persons who wait upon them in the tower and the twelve domestics mentioned above.

Dinner. For dinner the head cook provides three soups and two courses, consisting (on other than fast days) of four entrées, at least three of these and perhaps all being of meat, two roasts, four or five side dishes. Dessert: the steward generally adds by way of dessert a plate of pears, three compôtes, three plates of fruits, three rounds of butter, two kinds of sugar, a bottle of oil, a bottle of Champagne, a small decanter of Bordeaux, another of Malvoisie, another of Madeira, and seven rolls.

For those who dine on what remains, a two-pound loaf and two bottles of *vin ordinaire* are added.

Supper consists of three soups and three courses. On days other than fast days these consist of two entrées, two roasts, and four or five side dishes; on fast days [when Louis XVI fasted, but his family did not] of four entrées not made of meat, two or three of meat, two roasts, and four side dishes. Dessert, the same as for dinner, except for coffee.

Louis XVI's son generally has a little supper separately.

Members of the Paris Commune *took turns in watching for forty-eight hours in the apartments of the royal family. One of these guards was Charles Goret, formerly an inspector of market supplies:*

The first time I went into this prison, the queen, recognising me, came to me and said: 'We are very happy to see you.' The place had been newly decorated, if such an expression may be used in regard to a prison. The outer room, in which my colleagues and I sat—for at that time there were often at least two of us on guard—was hung with a paper intended to represent architecture. It opened into a little dining-room and the room occupied by the king. . . . Next to that was the room occupied by the princesses and the children, and beyond that was Cléry's [the valet-de-chambre's] room. All were nicely decorated and furnished. The windows, whose embrasures were about six feet deep, were furnished with strong iron bars and were screened outside, so that it was impossible to see into the prison from any of the high buildings opposite. The king and his family had lost much of the serenity I

30] Dinner for the royal family imprisoned in the Temple

had previously observed in them. The king walked back and forth, and wandered out from his own room to the one where we were sitting. Sometimes he would glance at the upper part of the window and ask what the weather was like; I saw him, too, look at a large board hanging on the wall of this room with the 'Rights of Man' inscribed on it. Having read what was on the board, the king said: 'That would be very fine if it were practicable.' The queen sat more quietly in her room, but Madame Elisabeth walked back and forth like the king, often with a book in her hand. The children came and went in the same manner. The appearance and behaviour of the whole family was very different from what I had observed before they were moved to these quarters. Everything seemed to presage the even greater misfortunes that we later witnessed. The father, wife, and sister were much more seldom together, and conversed much less frequently. It seemed as though they were afraid of aggravating their ills by speaking of them; and this is the saddest of all states, to be beyond the reach of consolation.

Despite the constant vigilance of their guards, the royal family still contrived to remain in touch with the outside world through the machinations of Louis-François

31] Louis XVI, three days before his execution

Turgy, one of their old kitchen staff who had succeeded in insinuating himself into the Temple. He told the Commune's *representatives that he had the assembly's permission, and the assembly's representatives that he had the* Commune's *permission and was allowed to remain:*

As soon as the king was removed to the Temple the most minute precautions were ordained. This was the routine in my own special province. Before dinner—or any other meal—someone went to the council room to summon two of the *Commune* officers. They came to the serving-room, where the dishes were prepared and tasted in front of them, so that they could see there was nothing concealed in them or anything suspicious about them. The decanters and coffee-pots were filled in their presence. Covers for the jugs of almond milk were made by whoever the officers directed to do it, from whichever piece of paper the officers chose.

Then we all proceeded to the dining-room, but we did not lay the table until the officers had scrutinized it above and below; we unfolded the table-cloths and napkins before them; they tore the rolls in half and probed the inside with forks or even with their fingers.

Nevertheless, I was often able, in one of the passages or at the bend of a staircase, to replace one paper jug-cover with another on which some warning or item of news had been written, either with lemon-juice or with extract of gall-nut. Sometimes I rolled a note round a little lead pellet, covered it with another piece of stronger paper, and dropped it into the jug of almond milk. I indicated what I had done by means of a sign we had agreed between us. When the paper stoppers had no writing already on them, the queen and Madame Elisabeth used them for giving me orders or information to pass on to someone else.

To the prisoners, the days passed slowly. Some years later, the Duchesse d'Angoulême —the king's daughter, and sole survivor of the little group in the Temple—told how they occupied their time in those last months of 1792:

My father always rose at seven o'clock, and prayed until eight. He then dressed himself and my brother, which occupied him until nine, when he came to breakfast in my mother's apartment. After breakfast, my father heard my brother's lessons, until eleven o'clock; my brother then played until twelve, at which hour we all went together to walk in the garden—no matter what the weather was—because it was necessary that the guard, which was relieved at that hour, should identify each of us, and be able to answer for our presence. We generally remained walking until two o'clock, when we went to dinner.

After dinner my father and mother played at trictrac or at piquet; or rather they pretended to play, in order to have an opportunity of saying a few words to each other. At four o'clock my mother came to us, and brought my brother with her, my father being in the habit of sleeping at that hour.

At six o'clock my brother returned to my father, who taught him his lessons, and allowed him to play until supper. At nine o'clock my mother undressed him and put him to bed, after which we all went to my mother's apartment, where we remained together until eleven, at which hour my father retired to rest. My mother was constantly employed in working at embroidery; she also directed my studies, and frequently made me read to her aloud. My aunt spent the greater part of her time praying, and always read the prayers of the day. She read a great number of books on piety, which my mother frequently asked her to read aloud.

The Death of the King

When the famous armoire de fer, *the metal cabinet containing the royal correspondence with Austria, was found in the Tuileries, it was the king's death-warrant. Austria was an enemy and Louis XVI was guilty of high treason against the nation.*

In the audience at the king's trial was a young Englishman of republican sympathies, Henry Redhead Yorke:

A wooden chair was brought, and Barère invited the king to be seated. He then read the whole of the charges, during which the king fixed his eyes upon him, but seemingly not with attention. From this circumstance, I did flatter myself (and there were many members of the Convention who also wished it) that, like Charles the First, he would either deny the competency of the tribunal to try him, or have appealed to the people. But he adopted neither the one nor the other. To every charge he answered directly, without pre-meditation, and with such skilful propriety that the audience were astonished; and this gave rise to an idle report, that Pétion had contrived to furnish him with a copy in the Temple. . . .

When he was accused of shedding the blood of Frenchmen, he raised his voice with all the consciousness of innocence, and in a very strong tone of indignation replied: 'No, sir! I have never shed the blood of Frenchmen.' His spirit was evidently wounded at this charge, and I perceived a tear trickle down his cheek. . . .

The king was plainly dressed in an olive silk coat, and looked remarkably well. Barère, the president, wore a dark mixture, a scarlet waistcoat, and a lead-coloured pair of kerseymore breeches, with white silk stockings. Pétion was elegantly dressed in black, as well as several of his party; Robespierre was also dressed in black. Orléans was habited in blue, and the majority of the members looked like blackguards.

There was no doubt of the king's guilt, but the penalty for his crime had yet to be decided. The Girondins in the new Convention found themselves in an invidious position. If they voted for the king's death, they would alienate the moderates among the newly elected and not yet committed deputies; if they voted for reprieve, they would betray all their well-publicized principles of earlier years. Furthermore, they would lay themselves open to Jacobin charges of royalism and treason. Brissot and Vergniaud tried to evade the issue by suggesting a referendum, but, in the end, after much backstairs intrigue, much buying and selling of votes, the deputies mounted the rostrum one by one to pronounce their verdict.

L.-S. Mercier, one of the Girondin deputies, looked back on the scene four years later:

The notorious session which determined the fate of Louis XVI lasted for seventy-two hours. You picture to yourself, no doubt, an atmosphere of thoughtfulness, silence, a sort of religious awe. Not at all. The far end of the room was transformed into a grandstand, where ladies in the most charmingly loose attire ate ices and oranges and drank liqueurs. We went to pay our respects; we returned to our place. The ushers played the part of attendants at boxes at the Opera. They were constantly to be seen opening the doors of the reserved galleries and gallantly showing in the mistresses of the Duc d'Orléans-Egalité, caparisoned with tricolour ribbons. . . .

32] The king bids farewell to his family and retainers

The public galleries during the days preceding this famous judgement were never less than crammed with foreigners, and people of every class; they drank wine and brandy as if they were in a tavern. The betting was open in every neighbouring café.

Boredom, impatience, weariness were imprinted on almost every face. Each deputy went in turn to the rostrum and everyone kept saying: 'Is it nearly my turn?' They brought in I know not which sick or convalescent deputy; he came muffled up in his nightcap and dressing-robe. The assembly laughed.

There passed the rostrum faces made more sombre by the pale gleam of the lights; in slow and sepulchral tones they uttered the one word 'death'. Picture all those countenances succeeding one another; all those voices; those different intonations; Orléans hooting, hissing, when he pronounced sentence of death on his kinsman; others calculating whether they would have time to dine before giving their verdict, while women pricked cards with pins to compare the totals; deputies who fell asleep and had to be wakened up to vote.

The verdict, by a single vote, was death without respite or reprieve. On 21 January 1793, Louis XVI went to his death on the scaffold.

The morning was bitterly cold and misty. The approach of the column was announced by a thundering roll of drums—it appeared to me that there must have been more than a hundred drummers; while now and then a flourish of trumpets added to the solemnity of the gloomy music of this unmelodious death-march. Thousands of National Guards, and *fédérés* [provincial troops] followed by the populace of the faubourgs, armed with pikes, and two brigades of field-pieces, preceded the immediate escort of the condemned monarch. The carriage he was in was nearly concealed by the mounted gendarmes that surrounded it, so that I could not catch a glimpse of his person.

33] The end, not of a man, but of an institution

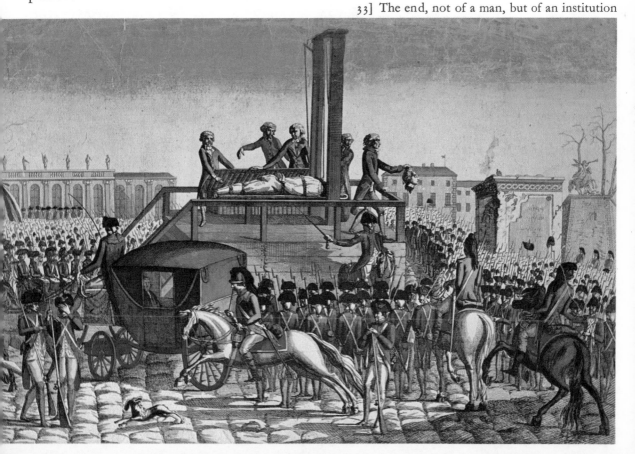

Such were the impressions of an English onlooker, J. G. Millingen, who was only a child at the time. Inside the carriage with the king was an Irish priest, the Abbé Edgeworth:

The coach arrived, amid a great silence, and stopped in the middle of a wide empty space which had been left round the scaffold; this space was edged with cannon; and beyond, as far as the eye could reach, was an armed multitude.

As soon as the king felt the coach coming to a stop, he leaned over to me and said in a whisper, 'We have arrived, if I am not mistaken.' My silence said yes. One of the executioners came forward to open the door of the coach, but the king stopped him and, putting his hand on my knee, said to the gendarmes: 'Messieurs, I commend this gentleman to your care; be good enough to see that after my death he is not offered any insult; I charge you to see to this.' As the gendarmes did not reply, the king began to repeat it in a louder voice, but he was interrupted by one of them saying: 'Yes, yes, we'll take care of that; leave it to us.' I must add that he said it in a tone of voice which would have frozen me, if at such a moment it had been possible for me to think of myself.

As soon as the king had got out of the coach, three of the executioners surrounded him, and tried to remove his outer garments. He pushed them away with dignity, and took off his coat himself. He also took off his collar and his shirt, and made himself ready with his own hands. The executioners, disconcerted for a moment by the king's proud bearing, recovered themselves, and surrounded him again in order to bind his hands. 'What are you doing?' said the king, quickly drawing his hands back. 'Binding your hands,' answered one of them. 'Binding me!' said the king, in a voice of indignation. 'Never! Do what you have been ordered, but you shall never bind me.' The executioners insisted; they spoke more loudly, and seemed about to call for help to force the king to obey.

This was the most agonizing moment of this terrible morning; one minute more, and the best of kings would have received an outrage a thousand times worse than death, by the violence that they were about to use towards him. He appeared to fear this himself, and turning his head, seemed to ask my advice. At first I remained silent, but when he continued to look at me, I said, with tears in my eyes: 'Sire, in this new outrage I see one last resemblance between Your Majesty and the God Who is about to be your reward.'

At these words he raised his eyes to heaven with an expression of un-utterable sadness. 'Surely', he replied, 'it needs nothing less than His example to make me submit to such an insult.' Then, turning to the executioners: 'Do what you will; I will drink the cup, even to the dregs.'

The steps of the scaffold were extremely steep. The king was obliged to lean on my arm, and from the difficulty they caused him, I feared that his courage was beginning to wane: but what was my astonishment when, arrived at the top, he let go of me, crossed the scaffold with a firm step, silenced with a glance the fifteen or twenty drummers who had been placed directly opposite, and in a voice so loud that it could be heard as far away as the Pont Tournant, pronounced these unforgettable words: 'I die innocent of all the crimes with which I am charged. I forgive those who are guilty of my death, and I pray God that the blood which you are about to shed may never be required of France.'

Mercier, who had voted against the death penalty, saw it carried out:

His blood flows. Cries of joy from eighty thousand armed men rend the air. The cries are repeated all along the quays. I see the pupils of the Collège des Quatre-Nations raising their hats on high. His blood flows, and there are people who dip a fingertip, a quill, a scrap of paper in it. There is one who tastes it, and says: 'It is vilely salt!' An executioner at the scaffold side sells small bundles of his hair; people buy the ribbon that tied it. Everyone carries off a small fragment of his clothing or some other blood-stained remnant from the tragic scene. I saw the whole populace go by, arm in arm, laughing, talking, as if returning from some festivity. . . . The day of execution made no impression; theatres were open as usual, and the taverns on the bloody square had their carafes emptied as usual. They cried cakes and patties round the decapitated body, which was put in the wicker basket of the common criminal. It was taken to the cemetery of the Madeleine and generously covered with quick-lime, so that it would be impossible for all the gold of the potentates of Europe to procure the smallest relic of his remains.

Ten days after the death of Louis XVI, France went to war with Britain—the country which, a century and a half before, had set the precedent in decapitating kings.

The Triumph of the Mountain

Within weeks, revolutionary France was at war with most of Europe; she also lost the second of her outstanding generals. At the end of 1792, La Fayette had fled to the Austrians; in April 1793, Dumouriez did the same. Another leading commander, Custine, was having to withdraw his troops in the Rhine area. To these military catastrophes was added economic distress, as a result of the cost of the war, and to economic distress was added civil strife, when the Vendée region of south-west France rose in arms against an attempt to enforce conscription.

There were food riots in Paris, and disturbances over the price and scarcity of various basic essentials, including soap. Restif de la Bretonne, on one of his evening walks in the city, saw several grocers' shops broken into and was moved to reflection:

It is agitators who have stirred up this imbecile people, these washerwomen soured by anxiety who, like animals, are aware only of the here and now, who feel for the grocer's wife—better tailored, better dressed—the same jealousy as a woman of the bourgeoisie used to feel for the advocate's or the counsellor's wife, as these in turn felt for the financier's wife and the lady of quality! The woman of the people believes she cannot do too much to bring the grocer's wife down to her level. She does not perceive that, if the grocer's wife is not more comfortably off, she will not be able to keep goods always in stock ready to sell; that, lacking such stock, she, the washerwoman, will often be obliged to wait until someone has gone to buy them; that she will lose a day's wages, time, and custom; that she will lack bread. None of all this enters her stupid head, and the agitators, the traitors who rouse her to action, take care not to tell her that she is working against herself.

As the value of the assignat went down and down, prices appeared to go up and up, giving the street-corner agitators who—as Restif surmised—were behind the riots more fuel to add to the fires of unrest. In May 1793, the Convention was forced to introduce the first law of the 'maximum' which attempted to control the supply and maximum price of grain. Tom Paine, the Anglo-American political philosopher who had been granted honorary French citizenship and elected to the Convention, wrote a didactic but penetrating letter to Danton on 6 May:

The people of Paris may say that they will not give more than a certain price for provisions, but as they cannot compel the country people to bring provisions to market, the consequence will be directly contrary to their expectations, as they will find dearness and famine instead of plenty and cheapness. They may force the price down upon the stock in hand, but after that the market will be empty. . . .

I am distressed to see matters so badly conducted, and so little attention paid to moral principles. It is these things that injure the character of the revolution, and discourage the progress of liberty all over the world. . . .

There ought to be some regulation with respect to the spirit of denunciation that now prevails. If every individual is to indulge his private malignancy or his private ambition, to denounce at random and without any kind of proof, all confidence will be undermined and all authority be destroyed.

This tendency to denunciation had been encouraged by recent legislation. In fact, most of the machinery of the Terror was set up while the Girondins were in control of the Convention. It should be explained here that France had no real government, as we understand the word today. There were no real political alignments, no real party policies. Each issue which came before the Convention was decided by a majority of those deputies present and voting. As a result, the process of government was often an inconsequent business. The Convention consisted of three perceptible units—the Girondins, the Jacobins (who, from their seats high up at the back of the chamber, came to be known as 'the Mountain'), and the main body of uncommitted deputies (who sat on the floor of the house, and are often referred to as 'the Plain'). The Girondins came mostly from provincial constituencies and therefore found it easier to win support from the provincial deputies of the Plain than did the Jacobins, whose main strength was in Paris.

During the period of Girondin supremacy, local watch committees were set up which were to become one of the main instruments of the Terror; the Committee of

34] Decree of the National Convention, setting up the Committee of Public Safety

Public Safety was formed; laws of increased severity against rebels, counter-revolutionaries, émigrés, and refractory priests were passed; a Revolutionary Tribunal was set up to sit in judgement on traitors. None of these measures was calculated to improve either the economic or the military situation. There, the Girondins were proving irresolute and incompetent. But their grip on the Convention did not relax. To their opponents, it was clear that the Girondins must be relieved of power—and quickly—if the country was to be saved; force was the only way this could be achieved.

Pétion, ex-mayor of Paris and a Girondin deputy, describes the first part of the confrontation:

The clouds gathered round our heads and the storm was about to break. The 31st of May was the day on which the conspiracy was to be sprung, on which the Convention was to be dissolved, on which certain victims were to fall to the assassins' steel. The lugubrious sound of the tocsin, the drums beating the general call, the closed barriers, the post messengers detained, the intercepted letters, the bloodthirsty motions proposed on the rostrums of the popular societies and repeated among numberless groups of people, the invasion of the Convention chamber—all these proclaimed a great catastrophe. What leaves no doubt that 31 May was the fatal day fixed by the conspirators is that they had, in advance, had seals engraved with the legend 'Revolution of 31 May', and they had the audacity to stamp and seal the letters that they opened, read, and finally passed on to the citizens to whom they were addressed. . . .

The conspirators, in spite of the gold they had poured out, in spite of their ringleaders, in spite of their anarchical preaching, in spite of the general call, the tocsin, the assembly of hirelings, could not stir up the movement to the pitch they required, and the *coup* failed.

In fact, the coup *had by no means failed. The Jacobins had carried the first of their demands within the Convention, by a majority of the Convention. No blood had been spilled, no heads broken. 1 June passed quietly enough. On 2 June, a deputation from the* Commune *went to the Convention and demanded the resignation or arrest of the*

35] Hérault de Séchelles confronted by Hanriot on 2 June 1

Girondin leaders. Towards the end of the day, the Convention tried to leave their chamber, without having reached a decision. Lanjuinais, one of the Girondin leaders, relates what happened when the deputies sallied forth with Hérault de Séchelles, the president, at their head:

The deputies advanced bare-headed; the president alone had his head covered, as a sign that the country was in danger; the Convention ushers preceded him; they demanded that a passage be opened [through the immense crowd outside].

Hanriot [who commanded the National Guard] comes forward on horseback with his aides-de-camp, and, pulling his hat over his forehead, draws his sabre: 'F . . .', he exclaims. 'You can't give orders here. Go back to your post, give up the deputies the people want.'

Some deputies insist; Hanriot draws back fifteen paces and cries: 'To arms! Gunners, stand to!' The troop under his command prepares for attack; there are even rifles trained on the deputies; the gunners seem to be preparing to put the match to their cannon; the hussars draw their sabres.

The president withdraws and presents himself, with the assembly, before all the successive companies in the courtyard and in the garden, without finding any exit.

However, the majority of the armed troops, their hats on the point of bayonet or pike, cried: 'Vive la république! Vive les députés! Peace, peace! Laws, laws! A constitution!' A small number shouted 'Vive la Montagne, vive les bons députés!' A still smaller number cried: 'To the guillotine with Brissot, Guadet, Vergniaud, Gensonné, Pétion, Gorsas, Barbaroux, Buzot etc. . . .' Others, still, cried: 'Purge the Convention; draw the bad blood.'

The deputies returned to their seats, where they agreed to a motion for the suspension and house arrest of twenty-nine Girondins. The Convention bowed, not to force, but to the threat of force. The Jacobins had won. Twenty of the twenty-nine suspended deputies evaded their house arrest and fled from Paris. Seventy-five other uncommitted, but nervous, deputies also forsook the city as well as the duties to which they had been elected.

The Beginning of the End

'What is it? What is it?', everyone was asking his neighbour.

'It's a murder.'

'Who's been murdered?'

They answered in an undertone. 'Marat.'

'Where was he murdered?'

36] The body
of the murdered
Marat

'In his bath.'

'Who did it?'

'A woman.'

'Has she been arrested?'

Some said 'no' with an air of suppressed delight. Others said 'yes' and fell silent again. One inquired discreetly if the wound was mortal.

'Where was he struck?'

'Below the right collarbone, between two ribs.'

'Was it a bullet?'

'No. A knife, driven into his lungs to the full length of the blade.'

'Plague on it! She must have struck hard.'

Thus the public executioner, Sanson, described the scene outside the home of Jean-Paul Marat on 13 July 1793. Marat, one of the wild men of the revolution, was suffering from a skin disease which only warm water seemed to relieve. For some weeks, he had spent much of the time immersed in his boot-shaped bath, with a vinegar-soaked towel round his head and a supply of paper and ink at his side so that he need never stop work. This was how Charlotte Corday—a twenty-four-year-old supporter of the Girondins, from Caen in Normandy—found him when she went to kill him.

Less than an hour after the murder, she was interrogated at the scene of the crime by Jacques-Philibert Guellard, police superintendent of the district.

GUELLARD: Required her to tell us what had decided her to attempt this assassination.

CORDAY: Replied that, having seen civil war about to flare up throughout France, and persuaded that Marat was the principal author of this disaster, she had chosen to sacrifice his life to save her country.

GUELLARD: Pointed out to her that it did not seem natural that she should have conceived this deplorable scheme of her own accord, and required her to tell us the persons she most commonly associated with in the town of Caen.

CORDAY: Replied that she had not told her plan to a living soul; that she had had the passport she used for coming to Paris for some time; that when setting out from Caen on Tuesday, and taking leave of the elderly relative at whose house she lived, she had merely said that she was going to see her father; that very few persons frequented the house of this relative; and that no one ever knew anything of her plan.

GUELLARD: Remarked that there seemed good reason to believe that she had left the town of Caen only to come and assassinate citizen Marat.

37] Charlotte Corday arrested

CORDAY: Replied that it was true she had this intention, and that she would not have left Caen if she had not meant to carry it out.

GUELLARD: Called upon her to tell us where she procured the knife which she used to commit the murder; to tell us who she had seen in Paris; and finally to give an account of what she had done in Paris since Thursday, when she arrived.

CORDAY: Replied that she bought the butcher's knife she used to assassinate Marat on the morning of the murder at eight o'clock, at the Palais Royal, and that she had paid forty sous for it. She knew no one in Paris, where she had never been before. Arriving on Thursday about midday, she went to bed. She only left her room on Friday morning to walk in the Place des Victoires and the Palais Royal. In the afternoon she did not go out, but busied herself with writing various papers which we would find on her person. This morning she had gone out to the Palais Royal between half past seven and eight o'clock and bought the knife we had already spoken of. She took a coach at the Place des Victoires to the home of citizen Marat, but was not able to see him. Back at home, she took the course of writing to him by the district post and, giving false reasons, asked him to see her. At half past seven in the evening, she took a coach to citizen Marat's to receive his reply to her letter. In case she met with a refusal, she had provided herself with another letter, which was in her pocketbook and which she intended to send in to citizen Marat. But she did not make use of it, as she was allowed in this time. She said finally that her plan was not at all an ordinary plan.

GUELLARD: Asked her how she had gained access to citizen Marat this second time, and at what point she had committed the crime against his person.

CORDAY: Replied that some women had opened the door to her, and had refused to let her in to see Marat, but that he—having heard the witness insisting—asked that she be brought in to where he was, in his bath. He had put several questions to her about the [Girondin] deputies now at Caen. . . . Marat said it would not be long before they were guillotined, and it was then that the witness drew the knife which she had hidden in her bosom and there and then struck the said Marat in his bath.

GUELLARD: Asked her if, after having accomplished the crime, she had not tried to escape by the window.

CORDAY: Replied no, she had no intention of escaping by the window, but she would have gone out by the door if she had not been stopped.

On the eve of the day on which she was to be judged and executed, Charlotte Corday wrote to her father, M de Corday d'Armont, at Argentan.

Forgive me, my dear Papa, for having disposed of my existence without your permission. I have avenged many innocent victims, I have prevented many other disasters. The people one day, undeceived, will rejoice to have been delivered from a tyrant. If I tried to make you believe that I was going to England, it was because I hoped to preserve my incognito; but I recognized that this was impossible. I hope that you will not be troubled. In any case, I believe that you will find friends at Caen. I have accepted Gustave Doulcet to defend me, but a crime of this kind permits of no defence. It is only for form's sake. Farewell, my dear Papa. I beg you to forget me or, rather, to rejoice at my fate. The cause of it is glorious. I embrace my sister, whom I love with all my heart, and all my relatives.

Do not forget Corneille's line:

'The crime makes the shame, and not the scaffold.'

Tomorrow at eight o'clock I am to be judged.

But instead of ending bloodshed, as she had believed, Charlotte Corday's act ushered in a new era in which the revolution began to consume its makers. Charlotte Corday killed Marat in July 1793. By the end of July 1794, all the great men of the revolution were dead—the moderates and the extremists, the honest men and a few of the dishonest ones, the able men and the colourful ones, the men to whom revolution was an intellectual exercise, and those to whom it was an emotional necessity. Some were ruthless, some a little mad, some merely unpleasant. None of them had any sense of humour, except perhaps Danton. The year of blood which began with the death of Marat washed away every man of stature and left behind a tide-wrack of nonentities, concerned only with self-preservation and self-advancement. When the girl from Normandy used her butcher's knife on Marat, she struck the first fatal blow at the revolution itself.

When she went to the scaffold, however, Charlotte Corday saw herself as a new St Joan, sacrificing her life to save her country. A German historian, Klause, was present at the event.

She looked on the surging multitude with ineffable sweetness, and when the people, wild with excitement, or groups of furies in women's guise, greeted her with strident shouts, one glance from her beautiful eyes was often enough to silence them. Her smile was the only outward sign of her emotions. As she approached the scaffold, she looked as if she was reaching the end of a tiring journey. She was alone. Without assistance, she climbed the steps of the bloodstained apparatus, and did not even change colour. Only when her neck was bared before the crowd did a more intense tint come to her virginal cheeks. Her noble head, her bare shoulders, the tranquil look which she cast round her, produced the most profound impression. Already half transfigured, she seemed an angel of light. She bowed courteously to the people round the scaffold and wished to address the public. This was not permitted. Then she approached the death-machine and, of her own accord, placed her head on the appointed spot. The plank subsided more slowly than usual. Solemn silence reigned. The fatal blade fell, and cut off the most beautiful of heads. . . . Thus ended Charlotte Corday, the sublime maiden of Caen.

38] The arrest and imprisonment of 'suspected persons' was decreed

The Last Days of Marie Antoinette

The murder of Marat, the rebellions in the countryside, the apparent imminence of foreign invasion—all these demanded of the new Jacobin rulers not only that action be taken, but that it be seen to be taken. Marie Antoinette was the unhappy symbol of all that threatened the revolution.

On 1 August 1793, the 'widow Capet' was transferred from the Temple to the Conciergerie, that fatal prison which was antechamber to the guillotine. Rosalie Lamorlière worked there as a servant to Madame Richard, wife of the jailer; she describes the queen's arrival.

The weather was hot. I noticed beads of sweat running down the queen's face, which she wiped two or three times with her handkerchief. Her astonished eyes took in the horrible emptiness of the room, and she looked with some attention at the jailer's wife and myself. Then, standing on an upholstered stool I had brought from my room, the queen hung her watch on a nail she had noticed in the wall and began to undress to go to bed. I went forward respectfully to offer her my assistance. 'No, thank you, my girl,' she replied, without any trace of either peevishness or pride. 'Since I have had no one to look after me, I look after myself.'

Daylight had come. We took away our candles and the queen lay down on

39] The 'widow Capet'. Marie Antoinette in the Conciergerie

a bed that was certainly quite unfit for her, but which we had at least provided with very fine linen and a pillow.

Within a few weeks, the queen's jailers were themselves imprisoned on suspicion of being implicated in a plot to free the queen. Their place was taken by the head jailer of the Force Prison, a man named Bault, whom Rosalie calls 'Lebeau'.

When Lebeau went to the queen's room for the first time, I went with him carrying the soup she usually had for breakfast. She looked at Lebeau who, as was the fashion of the day, wore the *carmagnole* [combined jacket and trousers]. The collar of his shirt was open and turned back, but his head was uncovered. His keys in his hand, he stood close to the wall near the door.

The queen removed her nightcap, took a chair, and said to me pleasantly: 'Rosalie, I want you to put up my chignon for me today.' Hearing these words, the jailer ran forward, seized the comb and, pushing me aside, said in a loud voice: 'Leave it alone, leave it alone; that is my business.' The queen, greatly surprised, looked at Lebeau with an air of supreme majesty and said: 'I thank you, no.' Then, rising to her feet, she did her hair herself and put on her cap. . . . Her Majesty took from the table the roll of white hair-ribbon that was left over and said to me, with an expression of melancholy affection that went straight to my heart: 'Rosalie, take this ribbon and keep it always in memory of me.' The tears came to my eyes and, as I thanked her, I curtsied.

When the jailer and I were in the corridor, he took my ribbon, and when we reached his room upstairs, he said: 'I am very sorry to have annoyed that poor woman, but my position is so difficult that the least thing makes me tremble. I cannot forget that my comrade Richard and his wife are in a prison cell. For God's sake, Rosalie, do nothing imprudent or I am a lost man. . . .'

She was liable to receive unexpected visits in her cell at any hour of the day or night. The architects and prison administrators kept coming to make sure that the iron bars and walls were perfectly secure. I could see they were perpetually on edge, and heard them asking each other: 'Could she not escape this way? Or that way?' They allowed neither us nor themselves a single moment of relaxation.

Their fear of treachery within or some surprise from outside kept them constantly round us in the Conciergerie. They ate their meals uninvited at the jailer's table, and every day I had to prepare quantities of food for fifteen or eighteen of these people.

On 14 October, the advocate Chauveau-Lagarde was in the country. There, a messenger came to him to inform him that he and one Tronçon-Ducoudray had been chosen to defend the queen, and that the trial would begin the following day at 8 a.m. There was no time to study the voluminous documents in the case, and an appeal for postponement elicited no response. In his account, Chauveau-Lagarde says:

The trial began at eight o'clock in the morning, continued without pause until four in the afternoon, was interrupted until five, and then went on until four o'clock the following morning. Thus, except for one brief interval of rest, it lasted for about twenty consecutive hours, during which a crowd of witnesses was examined one after the other.

Imagine, if you can, the will-power needed by the queen to bear the fatigues of a sitting as long and as horrible as this; to endure the stares of a whole crowd; to stand up against the monsters who thirsted for her blood; to escape the snares they laid for her; to overcome all their arguments; yet to remain within the bounds of propriety and moderation and never to be unworthy of herself.

Only those who witnessed every detail of this too notorious trial can have any real idea of the nobility of character which the queen showed on this occasion.

Question after question was asked Marie Antoinette about the part she had played in politics. She replied merely that she had acted as a good wife to her husband, the king; but no one was convinced. Charges of political conniving were reinforced by charges of personal immorality, which she met with impressive dignity.

One of her finest answers, to an odious question from one of the jurymen, produced a movement of admiration on the part of the crowd which for an instant interrupted the proceedings. She was aware of the impression she had made and signalled me to approach the steps within reach of her. In a low voice, she asked me: 'Did I not put too much dignity into my reply?' I answered: 'Madame, be yourself and you will always do what is best. But why do you ask?' 'Because', said the queen, 'I heard a woman say to her neighbour: "See how proud she is!"'

This showed that the queen still had hope. It showed, too, that her clear conscience permitted her to remain mistress of herself; amid all this mental turmoil, she heard everything that was said by those round her.

When the witnesses had all been examined, my colleague and I consulted for a moment on the best line to take in our speeches.

M Tronçon-Ducoudray undertook to defend the prisoner against the

] The interrogation of Marie Antoinette

charge of conspiring with enemies of the people in France, while I was to deal with the charge of conspiracy with foreign powers.

Hardly had we agreed this arrangement and given each other all the notes that might possibly bear on our respective tasks than, at the end of quarter of an hour, we were called back into the court and obliged to speak immediately, without preparation.

However great the talent that M Tronçon-Ducoudray showed in his address, however great the zeal I put into mine, there can be no doubt that our speeches for the defence were unworthy of such a cause. . . .

After pleading for two hours, I was overcome with fatigue, and the queen was good enough to notice this. 'How exhausted you must be, M Chauveau-Lagarde,' she said in the most touching manner. 'I am so very grateful for all your efforts.'

These words were heard by the people around her, including her enemies. The sitting was suspended for a moment before M Tronçon-Ducoudray began to speak and I tried to go to the queen, but in vain. A gendarme arrested me under her very eyes. As soon as M Tronçon-Ducoudray had finished pleading, he too was arrested in her presence. After that, we were not allowed to speak to her again.

The verdict was guilty. Early on the morning of 16 October, the queen returned to the Conciergerie to spend her last hours. Rosalie went to her to try and persuade her to eat something.

Her face was turned towards the window and her head was supported on her hand. 'Madame,' I said to her tremblingly, 'you ate nothing yesterday evening and hardly anything the whole day. What will you have this morning?' The queen's tears were flowing freely. She replied: 'I shall never need anything again, my child. Everything is over for me.' I dared to persist. 'Madame,' I said, 'I have kept some broth and some vermicelli on the range. You need sustenance. Let me bring you something.'

The queen's tears flowed afresh, but she said: 'Rosalie, bring me some broth.' I went to fetch it, and she sat up. But she could scarcely swallow more than a few mouthfuls. . . .

When daylight came, at about eight o'clock in the morning, I went back to Madame to help her dress, as she had told me to do when she was sitting on the bed drinking her broth. Her Majesty slipped into the narrow space I usually left between the bed and the wall. She unfolded a chemise they had probably brought to her when I was elsewhere and, signing to me to stand in front of the bed so as to hide her from the gendarme, she bent low behind the bed and slipped off her dress in order to change her underlinen for the last time. The gendarmerie officer immediately stepped forward and, standing by the head of the bed, watched what the queen was doing. Her Majesty quickly threw her *fichu* over her shoulders and, with the greatest gentleness, said to the young man: 'In the name of decency, monsieur, allow me to change my linen without being watched.'

'I cannot permit that,' the gendarme replied roughly. 'My orders are to keep an eye on you whatever you do.'

The queen sighed, slipped her chemise over her head for the last time taking all precautions to protect her modesty, and then put on not the long mourning dress she had worn before her judges, but the loose white gown she usually wore in the morning. Then, unfolding her large muslin *fichu*, she draped it round her neck and doubled it under her chin.

With her hair cut off at the back, and her hands tied behind her, the former queen of France went in a common tumbril to the place of execution. The Annual Register *described the event for its British readers.*

She seldom cast her eyes upon the populace, and regarded with indifference, if she at all regarded, the great armed force of thirty thousand men which lined the streets in double ranks. They who had seen her in the former part of her life could not but observe the altered state of her countenance, and what a sad change sorrow had made in that seat of animation and beauty. Her

41] The execution of the former queen of France

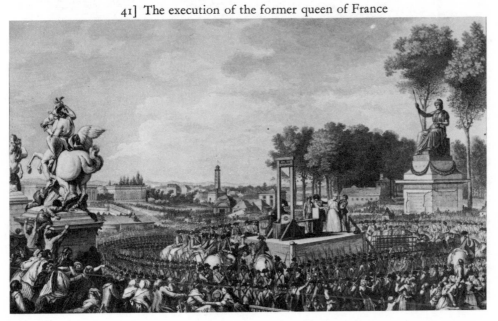

spirits appeared to be calm and she conversed with the priest who was seated by her with an air of decent submission but without the least appearance of anguish or dejection. She ascended the scaffold with much haste and seeming impatience, and then turned her eyes with apparent emotion towards the garden of the Tuileries, one of the scenes of her former greatness.

At half past twelve, the guillotine severed her head from her body, and the executioner exhibited it, all streaming with blood, from the four corners of the scaffold to an inveterate and insatiable multitude.

The Committee of Public Safety

After Marie Antoinette, it was the Girondins' turn to die. It is hardly profitable to speculate on what might have happened if they had accepted their defeat on 2 June in a rational and intelligent manner. What did happen was that many of them fled to centres of unrest in the provinces and did their best to encourage civil strife, hoping to

42] Condorcet poisons himself in prison

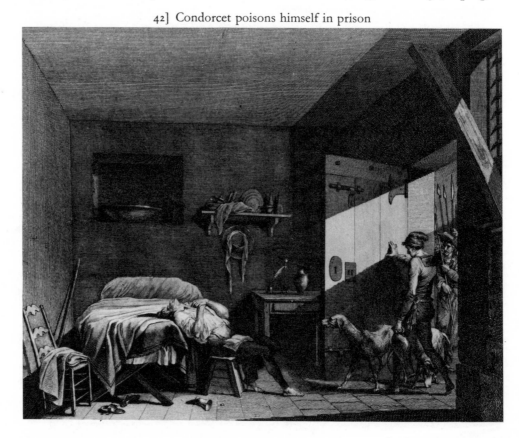

bring the Mountain crashing down, heedless of other consequences. At the end of October 1793, the Jacobin government staged a great show trial where twenty-one Girondins were condemned to the scaffold. The caption to a contemporary print records that all were guillotined within the space of thirty-six minutes.

Theirs was a merciful death compared with the misery suffered by some of their fellows. A few survived the revolution, many did not. Condorcet poisoned himself in prison; Pétion and Buzot, after months in hiding—when the first wrote his memoirs and the second a plea for vengeance—blew their brains out in a forest, and left their bodies to be eaten by dogs; and Roland, when he heard of the execution of his wife, walked out into a wild, wet night and stabbed himself to death.

But for the first time France had a real government, which set about stabilizing the country and reasserting central control over the provinces. Its determination, its authoritarianism, also began to turn the tide of war. The austerity imposed by war-time conditions, however, as well as by past inefficiencies, created an ideal climate for opposition. In Paris in February 1794, the inevitable food shortage resulted in incidents which were reported to the government by 'observers' of the ministry of the interior:

4 ventôse [22 February 1794]

The appearance of Paris begins to become alarming. In the markets and streets you meet a large crowd of citizens running, bumping into each other, shouting, weeping, everywhere presenting the image of despair. Seeing all this, you would imagine Paris already a prey to the horrors of famine.

15 ventôse [5 March 1794]

When a cart loaded with beans arrived at a grocer's door in the rue de Bretagne, Temple section, a considerable crowd of women and men, doubtless ill-disposed, rushed on these vegetables with such avidity that the guard was driven off and disarmed, and all was pillaged. But few persons paid for what they took.

21 ventôse [11 March 1794]

A number of people complain, and proclaim loudly that they have not tasted meat for a fortnight and that artisans have not the strength to work. I depose that it is urgent to forbid aristocrats having several dishes at a meal, for there are still some who have three or four.

At the end of March—led by Hébert, the editor of Père Duchesne—the men who stimulated and fed on the people's distress, the street-corner agitators, the wild men who screamed for the downfall of a too-Puritan government, the anarchists were ruthlessly suppressed, to the regret of no one. But then, as the deputy Levasseur relates:

Two days after the execution of the Hébertists, which Danton had so powerfully contributed to bring about, this same Danton was arrested during the night. . . . The Convention was filled with consternation at hearing the news. We already knew that Danton and Robespierre were forever at variance, but we thought Danton too strong by reason of his services and the support of the vast majority of his colleagues to be other than safe from the vengeance of his enemy. . . . We thought especially that the Committee of Public Safety understood how essential Danton and Camille [Desmoulins] were to the triumph of the cause of liberty, as much for their talent as for the influence of their well-known patriotism. Vain hope! The influential members of the committee, Robespierre and Saint-Just, did not know how to retreat from the application of their theories; to dispute one of their ideas was to declare oneself their enemy and, with them, the struggle could only end in death.

Danton's fall was brought about largely by his long association with financiers and speculators. Until the Committee of Public Safety (which was now in effect the inner council of the government) took a hand in the matter, the world of finance had been making much profit out of the fall in assignats *and the competition for vast war contracts. As a result of the committee's action, many of Danton's friends were now imprisoned. Since it would have been difficult to prove their innocence, Danton adopted different tactics—he called for a relaxation of the rule of force, 'the Terror'. France, he warned, was becoming a police state. This was all very well in times of emergency, but the military situation had improved and the Terror was no longer necessary. Basically, Robespierre agreed with Danton in this and, to begin with, supported him. Indeed, even the government's 'observers' were aware of the 'police state' atmosphere.*

1 pluviose [24 January 1794]

Calumny is still the order of the day. It is desirable to have a special law against those whose venomous lips cast the poison of calumny on everything around them, so as to take away, not life, but honour, reputation, trust, etc. These monsters think to make themselves shine at the expense of the innocent by representing them as moderates, aristocrats, federalists [de-centralizers], etc.—in short, sullying with a poisonous dye the reputations of the citizens they attack.

2 ventôse [20 February 1794]

This silence [in a much-frequented Paris café] is vexatious. It can arise only from two causes—either from the aristocracy, who know that their talk would not be allowable, or from timidity and distrust on the part of patriots who are generally outspoken, lest some malicious person should profit by an unguarded expression to accuse them, and to represent them as guilty in spite of their innocence.

Soon, however, it became painfully apparent that there might be too much support for

The Fête of the Supreme Being, 8 June 1794

Danton's campaign. A slight relaxation of the rule of force might have been possible; complete relaxation was out of the question. Robespierre withdrew his support, and although, at first, he made some attempt to save Danton and Desmoulins, he finally gave in to the more bloodthirsty members of the Committee of Public Safety—whose apparent head he was, but where he very often found himself outvoted.

On 5 April, telling the executioner, 'Don't forget to show my head to the people, it's worth it,' Danton died.

For some time, religion had been one of the great divisive forces of the revolution and 'refractory' Catholic priests had been responsible for much unrest in the countryside. Robespierre, a staunch follower of Rousseau, believed that religion was essential to the state; but it must be a tolerant religion, a religion freed from the old Catholic–Protestant antipathies, a religion freed from the 'superstitious' dogma of Rome. The new cult of the Supreme Being was to be a secular one; in short, it was to be the Christian way of life without the Christianity. On 8 June a splendid fête was held to inaugurate the new religion. The deputy Vilate describes how Robespierre looked to the assembled multitude on that glorious summer day:

With what arrogant delight, walking at the head of the National Convention, surrounded by an immense throng responding to the clear and shining brilliance of such a beautiful day with the elegance of their attire, he stalked along . . . wearing the tricolour scarf of the representatives of the people, his head shaded by flowing plumes. Everyone observed his intoxication; but while the crowd, carried away, uttered resounding cries of 'Vive Robespierre!' . . . his colleagues, alarmed at his bold pretensions, embarrassed his ears—as he complained later—with satirical asides and cutting remarks: 'Do you see how they are applauding him? Doesn't he want to play God? Isn't he the high priest of the Supreme Being?'

The magnificent spectacle had been arranged in the most minute detail by the painter Jacques-Louis David. During the early part of the ceremony, Robespierre was to set a torch to a large statue of Atheism, whose veil would then dissolve to reveal the figure of Wisdom, 'calm and serene'. Afterwards, according to David's plan (which was followed to the letter):

Amid the people, their representatives appear; they are surrounded by Childhood, adorned with violets; Adolescence, with myrtle; Virility, with oak; and white-haired Age, with vine and olive leaves. Each representative carries in his hand a bouquet of ears of corn, of flowers and of fruits, symbol of the task which has been confided to him; a task which they will carry out despite the obstacles which ever and again spring up beneath their feet.

In the centre of the national representatives, four strong bulls, festooned and garlanded, drag a chariot on which there sparkles a trophy constructed of instruments of the arts and crafts and products of French territory. 'You who live in luxury and indolence; you whose existence is only a troublesome slumber; perhaps you will dare to cast a glance of contempt at these service-able instruments. Ah! Fly, fly far from us. Your corrupted souls would not know how to savour the simple pleasures of nature! And you, industrious and sensitive people, rejoice in your triumph and in your glory. . . .'

An immense mountain becomes the altar of the nation; on its summit rises the tree of liberty; the representatives dart forward under the protection of its boughs; fathers with their sons group themselves on that part of the mountain which has been assigned to them; mothers with their daughters range them-selves on the other side. . . .

The young girls toss towards heaven the flowers which they have brought, their only property at so tender an age. At the same instant, and all at once, the boys—aflame with warlike ardour—draw their swords and place them in the hands of their aged fathers; they swear to make them everywhere victorious; they swear to bring about the triumph of equality and liberty over tyrannical oppression.

Two days after this splendid pageant, the Convention passed the edict known as 'the law of 22 prairial', which allowed the Revolutionary Tribunal to pronounce either of only two verdicts—acquittal or death. Two days after this splendid pageant when the nation dedicated itself to Wisdom 'calm and serene', the climax of the Terror began.

The Terror

The Terror can be divided into two phases. The first lasted from March 1793 until 10 June 1794; during this period 1251 people were executed in Paris. The second was much shorter: between 10 June 1794, when the Revolutionary Tribunals were reorganized, and 27 July 1794, when Robespierre fell, there were 1376 deaths on the scaffold. Thus even at its height, the Terror claimed only four more victims each day than Britain's roads in 1965. In the whole period, fewer people died than were mistakenly *condemned to face a French firing squad during the First World War. But such comparisons, though illuminating, are not altogether valid. They take no account of the atmosphere that prevailed in a city where, every day for almost seven weeks, more than a score of dripping heads were displayed on the scaffold.*

Among those who died were Philippe-Egalité, who had once hoped for the throne; Madame du Barry, Louis XV's autocratic mistress; Madame Elisabeth, Louis XVI's

A revolutionary committee under the Terror

45] The king's sister on the scaffold

autocratic sister; Lavoisier, France's greatest scientist; and André Chénier, who might have become one of France's greatest poets.

Not all those who were accused were condemned. And even of those who were condemned, some survived long enough to outlast the Terror and win reprieve. One such was an Englishman, Sir William Codrington, who was imprisoned in the Conciergerie:

Two of us procured the seventeenth part of a small apartment. The beds were placed so near together that one was obliged to get in at the feet; and though we paid for them apart, it was three weeks before I could get any sheets; and when at last I had them, I could with great facility have crept through them. But the room being very small and the ceiling so very low, and so many persons stove in so narrow a compass, the air was so bad we could none of us sleep, at least not for more than an hour, often less, and sometimes not at all.

As we were locked up every evening about five o'clock, and the door not opened until near ten the next morning, a tub was placed in the room. . . . We had with us a tolerably good physician, who advised us to burn incense every night before we went to bed, in order to purify the air, and to take a mouthful of brandy every morning as soon as we got up, as a preventive against infection. We all of us rose in the morning with a great dryness in the throat or something of a soreness. At twelve o'clock every night we used to be visited by three or four turnkeys, with as many great dogs. With large staves they used to thump against the ceiling, open the windows, and with an iron hammer beat against the bars to see that all was safe and sound. . . .

Four months I passed in this pleasing abode, having seen half my room companions quit me to take their final leave; and the half of that half have since shared the same fate.

Among the other prisoners in the Conciergerie during the first period of the Terror were Madame Roland and Comte Beugnot, an advocate. Beugnot describes the strange mixture of squalor and elegance which constituted daily life in such a place:

The authorities flung without distinction on the same straw and behind the same bolts the Duchesse de Gramont and a stealer of handkerchiefs, Mme Roland and some wretched streetwalker, a nun and a denizen of the Salpétrière. This lack of discrimination was a cruel infliction for the women of good class in that it exposed them to the daily spectacle of disgusting and horrible scenes. Every night we were awakened by the screams of women trying to tear each other to pieces. The room occupied by Mme Roland had become a haven of refuge in the midst of this hell. When she came down to the courtyard, her presence was enough to restore order and the women, whom no known power was able to master, refrained from misconduct for fear of displeasing her. To the poorest prisoners she gave money, and to all advice, consolation, and hope. As she moved about, these women clustered round her as though she were their tutelary goddess—very different from that dirty courtesan, the du Barry, who brought shame on Louis XV and his century, and who was then confined in the same prison. The common women treated her with ruthless equality, though she still preserved the wanton air and proud bearing of an august whore.

On the day on which Mme Roland was to appear before the court . . . she had dressed herself with care and was wearing an English-style costume of white muslin trimmed with net and gathered up with a black velvet sash. She had done her hair carefully and wore a simple but elegant bonnet, from beneath which her beautiful hair flowed on to her shoulders. Her face seemed more animated than usual, her complexion was brilliant and her lips wore a smile. With one hand she was attending to the train of her skirt, while she made over the other to a crowd of women who clustered round her to kiss it. Those who realized that she was going to her death sobbed and commended her to Providence. It would be impossible to do justice to the scene. One had to be there. Mme Roland addressed each one with affectionate kindness. She did not promise to come back, nor did she tell them she was going to her death, but her last words took the form of touching appeals to them. She urged them to be at peace with one another, to be brave, not to abandon hope and to practise the virtues which accord with misfortune. An old jailer named Fontenay, whose kind heart had survived thirty years of his cruel profession, wept as he opened the grille to her.

Our favourite walk, and indeed our only one, was along the corridor. We went down there as soon as they let us out of our cells. The women joined us somewhat later, as the claims of dress were overriding. In the morning they appeared in attractive négligé, the materials of which were matched with such freshness and grace that to judge from the general effect it was impossible to believe that the wearer had passed the night on a pallet or more probably on a heap of filthy straw. As a general rule, the women of the world who were brought to the Conciergerie kept alive to the last the sacred fires of good form and good taste. After appearing in the morning in négligé, they went up to their rooms and at noon one saw them coming down again tastefully arrayed and with their hair elegantly dressed. Their demeanour, too, had changed. Their movements were marked by greater emphasis and a kind of dignity. In the evening they appeared in undress. I noticed that almost all the women who could do so stuck to the rule of three costumes per day. The others made up for their lack of elegance by a cleanliness facilitated by local conditions, for the women's courtyard possessed a treasure in the shape of a fountain which gave them as much water as they needed. Every morning, I used to gaze at these unhappy creatures, who had brought with them no change of linen, busily engaged round the fountain in washing, laundering, and drying their solitary garment in noisy rivalry. The first hour of the day was dedicated to these duties from which nothing, not even the arrival of a warrant, would have deterred them.

Good Catholics died less regretfully when a priest had been able to give them absolution. To carry out this last duty, the Abbé Carrichon—in constant danger of being recognized and arrested—followed the tumbril of the ladies of the Noailles family:

The storm was at its wildest, and the wind was blowing strongly. The ladies in the first cart were greatly inconvenienced, especially the Maréchale de Noailles. Her bonnet blew back on her head, showing her grey hair. She staggered on the wretched floor with no hand-rail, her hands tied behind her back.

At once many of the people collected there recognized her and paid no heed to anyone else. They added to her torment by their insulting cries which she endured patiently. 'There she is, look at her! That's the marshal's wife who used to run such a fine show and drive in her grand carriages. Now she has to drive in the cart just like the others.' Nothing could be more insulting to a sensitive person than these cannibal cries. The unhappy should be treated as sacred objects, especially when they are innocent. The cries continued and the rain fell, more heavily than ever.

We had just reached the square before you come into the Faubourg St-Antoine. I went ahead, took my bearings, and said to myself: 'This is the best place to grant them what they most desire.' The cart had slowed down; I stopped and turned towards it, making a signal to Mme de Noailles, which she understood perfectly. She said, 'Mama, M. C. is going to give us absolution.' They immediately bowed their heads with an expression of piety, repentance, joy, and tenderness, which was balm to me. I raised my hand and with covered head pronounced the complete formula of absolution and the words which follow, very distinctly and with intense concentration. I felt that they were at one with me more than ever. I shall never forget this scene worthy of a Raphael's paintbrush.

From that moment the storm began to abate and the rain to decrease. It seemed to have been sent expressly by Providence to further the success of our plan.

Unavoidably, the place of execution provided something of a spectacle. People who lived near by—if it was to their taste, and if they could afford to forego a day's wages—turned up to watch the fun. When F.-M. de Kerverseau, a Parisian, returned to his native city after some months' absence and found he needed two character witnesses if he was to be allowed to remain, he went to see a tobacconist who had a profitable sideline in such testimony:

When I entered this little hole of a place, I found a woman sitting by a sort of counter, waiting, it seemed, for customers to whom to sell salt and tobacco, the only articles in which she dealt and of which she kept a very small supply. I asked her where her husband was as I had to speak to him. She replied that he would soon be back and that I would not have long to wait. He had only gone to the Place de la Révolution to see a score and a half of aristocrats 'sneezing into the sack'. That was the phrase with which Hébert described, in a foul rag entitled *La Grande Colère du Père Duchesne*, the amputation of heads, which, severed by the blade of the guillotine fell speedily one on top of another into a kind of basin, where they floated in blood, which splashed up as the heads dropped, and flooded the pavement of the place dedicated to these daily

46] A prison cell during the Terror. One of its inmates, M de Loizerolles offers his own life in return for his son's

butcheries. 'I told him,' she said, 'that it wasn't worth while going over there for such a small number and advised him to stay in the shop.'

As she had promised, her husband returned very soon. I explained to him the object of my visit. He appeared perfectly willing to act as my witness, and merely added that I should need another, adding, 'Oh! I shall find one soon enough. Perhaps you have not dined.' 'No,' I said. 'Well sit down on that stool; we'll have a drink and after that I'll settle your business.' 'Gladly,' I said, 'but on condition that I stand the wine.' 'Very good: I'll send the wife to fetch us something to eat.' As he ate, my tobacconist, who had witnessed the 'sneezing into the sack' reproached his wife for having tried to keep him at home and said that if he had listened to her he would have missed a great pleasure as he had never laughed so much.

From the story which he told us and to which I had to listen without flinching, I learnt that the individuals who had provided the comedy were none other than one of the executioner's valets and the coachman of the member of the Revolutionary Tribunal who went every day to the place of execution with the persons condemned by the tribunal in order to witness their death and provide legal proof of the same. Now, as the guillotine was always ready from a quarter of an hour to an hour before the arrival of the condemned persons, one of the executioner's valets who had been helping to set it up, amused himself by dancing round the instrument as soon as it was in position, and by his capers, antics, and grimaces entertained the crowd before providing them with the more substantial pleasure of seeing heads fall. As for the coachman, he was not a whit less comical than the other fellow. The judge's carriage always preceded the carts carrying the condemned. The coachman announced to the crowd by his gestures that the aristocrats were coming, that they were here and that they would soon be putting their heads into the noose. The coachman, grotesquely arrayed in a red bonnet and a *carmagnole* of the same colour, leapt down from the box and sprang back again with a single bound. When the condemned were numerous he showed great pleasure and it appears that his gaiety was proportionate to the number of heads to be lopped off. However, although on this occasion there were only thirty, he seemed to be in particularly good form, as my companion kept exploding with laughter at the recollection. 'By God,' he said, after concluding his narrative, 'these dogs died very bravely. It's unfortunate that the aristocrats die like that.'

] The last victims of the Terror await the call to the guillotine

It should, however, be emphasized that for the majority of Parisians the atmosphere might be uneasy, but life went on more or less as usual. In days before public transport and mass communications, in a city whose streets were narrow and where each district was almost as self-contained as a village, news did not travel fast. There might be a riot in one area, without another district hearing of it until days afterwards, if at all. Early in the revolution, the inhabitants of the Faubourg St-Antoine district gained a reputation for extremism; the Faubourg St-Michel was also notoriously active. Thus, when eye-witnesses refer, as they so often do, to 'the faubourgs' advancing with pikes and cudgels, they do not necessarily mean 'the people of Paris'. They often mean groups of inhabitants united by local and specific interests or loyalties.

It was only when the guillotine turned its attention from aristocrats and priests to shopkeepers, clerks, and clockmakers, to the inhabitants of the faubourgs, in fact, that Paris as a whole became actively frightened and began to withdraw its backing from the government which ruled through force. When Robespierre most needed help from the Parisians who had for so long been his support, it was not forthcoming.

The Fall of Robespierre

The climax was swift and startling, although it followed upon weeks of subterranean intrigue. By early June, according to his sister, Charlotte, Robespierre had become convinced that certain members of the Committee of Public Safety were anxious to perpetuate the Terror for the sheer pleasure of it. He believed, says Charlotte, that:

This violent state had been necessary to frustrate the plots of the aristocrats and the agents of Pitt and Cobourg; but once the enemies of the revolution were vanquished, it was essential to put a limit to the severities which the country's dangers had necessitated. The era must come when legal order would succeed the revolutionary régime. This era Maximilien Robespierre believed had arrived. He wished, therefore, to fill in the pit [where guillotined bodies were buried] and substitute leniency for harshness. But his colleagues on the committee did not see matters in that way; Collot d'Herbois and Billaud-Varenne, in particular, wanted to make the Terror permanent or at least to prolong it indefinitely.

Other members of the committee would have been happy to see an end to the Terror, but they were at odds with Robespierre and Saint-Just over the conduct of the war. At this crucial time, when the Committee of Public Safety was divided—and when Robespierre himself was therefore vulnerable—he contrived to have recalled from the provinces several deputies who had been in charge of repression there, and who had carried out their duties with ghoulish enthusiasm. Charlotte takes up the story again:

His enemies blamed him for having sent bloodthirsty pro-consuls to the departments—though, on the contrary, it was he who arranged for the recall of almost all those who abused their limitless powers by practising atrocious cruelties; it was he who constantly wrote to the people's 'representatives on

48] Robespierre, having run out of victims, executes the executioner

mission' that they should be sparing of harshness, that they should make the revolution loved instead of loathed. Several times he demanded, without being able to obtain it, the recall of Carrier, who was protected by Billaud-Varenne. He was more successful in the case of Fouché.

I was present at the meeting Fouché had, on his return, with Robespierre. My brother demanded from him an account of the blood he had caused to be shed, and upbraided him so forcefully for his conduct that Fouché was pale and shaking. He stammered out a few excuses and blamed the gravity of the circumstances for the cruel measures he had taken. Robespierre told him that nothing could justify the cruelties he had been guilty of. Lyon, it was true, had been in a state of insurrection against the National Convention, but this was no excuse for the mass shooting of disarmed enemies.

From that day, Fouché was the most irreconcilable enemy of my brother and joined the faction which was plotting his downfall.

Joseph Fouché, in terror of his own life, was wily, vindictive, and single-minded in his instinct for self-preservation. Many years after, he told the tale with pride. Robespierre, he claimed, envisaged one more coup *which would make him master of the revolution:*

But thirty heads were still needed. He had marked them in the Convention. He knew that I had divined it, and that I also had the honour to figure in his notebook in the list of the condemned . . . I did not waste time arguing for my head or deliberating lengthily, in secret conclave, with those of my colleagues threatened as I was. It was enough for me to say to them—to Legendre, to Tallien, to Dubois-Crancé, to Daunou, to Chénier, among others—'You are on the list! You are on the list as I am, I am sure of it! . . .'

I went straight to those who shared the government of the Terror with Robespierre, and who I knew to be envious or fearful of his immense popularity. I revealed to Collot d'Herbois, to Carnot, to Billaud-Varenne, the plans of this modern Appius, and I drew each of them such a forcible and accurate picture of the danger of their position, I roused them so aptly and shrewdly, that I injected more into them than defiance—the courage to oppose themselves henceforward to letting the tyrant decimate the Convention any further. 'Count the votes in your committee,' I said to them, 'and you will see that, when you want it enough, he will be reduced to an impotent minority with Couthon and Saint-Just. Refuse him your vote; reduce him to isolation by your passive resistance. . . .'

What was his astonishment, how incensed he was, when he met insuperable opposition to his bloodthirsty scheming against the national representation! It has been too much mutilated already, they said to him. It is time to finish with this regular toll, which will end by claiming us too.

Seeing the majority vote escape him, he withdrew, filled with rage and vexation, swearing that he would not set foot again in the committee as long as his will was ignored there.

For almost four weeks out of the seven which formed the peak of the Terror, Robespierre did not set foot in the Committee of Public Safety or in the Convention. He kept himself in isolation, meditating his next move. It was a fatal delay. He was in opposition to the majority of members of the Committee of Public Safety, he was feared by many members of the Convention—for his cold puritanism, his political sagacity, his devoted following in the unruly Paris Commune, *and because they suspected that the law of 22 prairial might be turned against them—and he was hated by the other government committee (the Committee of General Security) whose special province was the police, and which was responsible for many of the arrests and executions generally ascribed to the more famous Committee of Public Safety. Fouché and his friends spent four weeks working on all these various fears, so that they might bring down Robespierre and save their own heads.*

When, on 26 July, Robespierre returned to the Convention and denounced his enemies, he spoke only in general terms. It was to be left to Saint-Just, the next day, to name names. But overnight, all the fears crystallized. Who was it to be, every deputy wondered. Me?

Saint-Just rose to speak on 27 July (9 thermidor), and chaos broke out. No one would give him a hearing. Robespierre tried to speak, and was howled down. He and a small band of his followers were arrested and dispatched to jail. The conspirators flattered themselves that they had won, but Robespierre still had the Paris Commune *behind him. He and his associates—his brother Augustin, Saint-Just, Couthon, Lebas— were released and went to the Hôtel de Ville. The* Commune's *army gathered to protect them, but as time wore on, as Hanriot (its commander) failed to give orders, as nothing appeared to be happening, as people heard that Robespierre had been outlawed by the Convention, the troops simply melted away. When Barras arrived from the Convention, with a hastily recruited force of six thousand men, to re-arrest Robespierre, it was the end. The end of Robespierre, the end of the Jacobins, the end of the Terror, the end of the revolution.*

Among the Convention forces was a renegade gendarme from the Commune, *Charles-André Méda:*

The *Commune* staircase is full of the conspirators' supporters; we can hardly get by, three abreast. Very excited, I run quickly up and am at the door of the *Commune* assembly room while the grenadiers are still far behind. The conspirators are gathered in the secretariat. . . . I see about fifty men in a state of great agitation; the sound of the artillery had taken them by surprise.

In the centre of them, I recognize Robespierre the elder. He is seated in an armchair, his left elbow on his knees and his head leaning on his left hand. I jump at him and, pointing my sabre at his heart, I say to him: 'Give yourself up, traitor!' He raises his head and tells me: 'It is you who are the traitor, and I am going to have you shot!' At these words, I take one of my pistols in my left hand and, transferring it to the right, I fire. I meant to strike him in the chest, but the bullet hits his chin and breaks the left lower jaw. He falls from his chair. The report of my pistol startles his brother—who throws himself out

49] Robespierre arrested in the Hôtel de Vi

of the window. At this moment, a frightful noise breaks out around me. I cry 'Vive la république!', my grenadiers hear me and respond. Then the confusion is complete amongst the conspirators and they disperse in all directions. I remain master of the scene. . . .

Robespierre and Couthon [who was injured while trying to escape] are stretched out at the foot of the rostrum. I search Robespierre, I take his pocketbook and his watch, and give them to Léonard Bourdon [a Convention deputy] who comes in at this moment to congratulate me on my victory and to give instructions about law and order.

Between one and two in the morning, Robespierre was carried on a plank to the Committee of Public Safety and laid on a table in the room adjoining the committee room. The deputy Courtois was later to produce a report on the events of 9 and 10 thermidor:

A deal box containing some samples of regulation bread from the army of the north was placed under his head as a kind of pillow. He remained for almost an hour in a state of immobility which suggested that he would soon cease to be. At last, after an hour, he began to open his eyes. The blood flowed plenteously from the wound he had in his left lower jaw. This jaw was broken and his cheek was pierced with a bullet-wound. His shirt was covered with blood. . . . About three to four in the morning, it was observed that he had a small white leather bag in his hands, on which was written: 'Au Grand-Monarque, Lecourt, sword-cutler to the king and his troops, rue St-Honoré near the rue des Poulies, Paris'; and on the back of the bag was: 'M. Archier's'. He made use of this bag to remove the clotted blood which came from his mouth. The citizens surrounding him watched his every movement; some of them even gave him some white paper (in default of linen), which he used for the same purpose, employing his right hand only and leaning on his left elbow. . . .

About six in the morning, a surgeon who was in the courtyard of the Palais National was called to dress his wounds. He took the precaution of putting a key in his mouth. He found that the left jaw was shattered. The surgeon extracted two or three teeth, bound up the wound, and put a bowl of water at his side. Robespierre made use of it from time to time, and wiped out the blood which filled his mouth with pieces of paper which he doubled over several times, using his right hand only. When it was least expected, he sat up, pulled up his stockings, slipped abruptly down from the table, and sat himself hurriedly in an armchair. Hardly was he seated than he asked for water and some white linen. All the time he was lying on the table after he recovered consciousness, he had been gazing fixedly at the people around him, and especially at the employees of the Committee of Public Safety whom he recognized. He often raised his eyes to the ceiling, but apart from a few convulsive movements it was noticeable that he remained quite impassive even when his wounds were being dressed, which must have given him acute pain. His complexion, always bilious, was as livid as death.

Robespierre's last hours were agonizing enough to satisfy even the most implacable of his enemies. But who actually did fire the shot that broke his jaw? Was it the gendarme Méda? The picture of him juggling with sabres and pistols is hardly convincing; it is even more suspect in view of the surgeon's report, which stated that Robespierre's wounds were caused by a pistol loaded, not with a bullet, but with small shot. Was it Robespierre himself? This is the view most historians accept, although both the deed itself and the inefficiency with which it was carried out are quite uncharacteristic. Furthermore, the angle of the shot suggests another hand than Robespierre's. The evidence for suicide rests on the testimony of a rather dubious eye-witness; it was, however, a gift to the propagandists—the villain at bay, the enemy of the people attempting to kill himself rather than face the just vengeance of the people! The third possibility is that it was Augustin Robespierre, hysterically intent on saving his brother from that same vengeance. Did Augustin snatch up the second pistol belonging to Lebas (who had succeeded in killing himself with the first), did he fire it at his brother, then, thinking him dead, did he try to kill himself by jumping out of the window? No one knows. Augustin lived long enough to be guillotined, but he was too weak to answer more than a very few questions. Robespierre himself was unable to speak. The only sound he uttered on the last day of his life was a 'tigerish cry' of pain when the executioner tore away his bandages on the scaffold where he and twenty-one of his followers perished.

The Whiff of Grapeshot

Robespierre and his twenty-one followers died on 10 thermidor. Another seventy-one members of the Commune *went to the guillotine the day after, the bloodiest day of slaughter in the whole revolution.*

The unholy alliance of convinced terrorists and frightened moderates who had brought Robespierre down had been acting against the man, not the system. But the main body of the Convention, and the people of Paris, did not distinguish between the two. There was a vast upsurge of anti-Terror reaction, which showed itself in the massacre of Robespierrist sympathizers—real or imagined—by bands of armed thugs who ranged the streets of the capital. In face of this, the country's rulers donned a snow-white mantle of innocence and blamed all that had gone before on the little lawyer from Arras, the small, trim, inflexible, incorruptible Robespierre. Soon there was a further purge of those whose hands were stained with the blood of the Terror; Collot d'Herbois, Billaud-Varenne, Barère, Carrier, Fouquier-Tinville—all were guillotined or deported to the penal colony of Guiana.

The Thermidorians (as the victors of 9 thermidor were called) set about dismantling all the administrative machinery which had made the Terror possible, while the people of Paris continued to starve and riot and run to arms.

In October 1795, Paris rose for the last time. The outgoing Convention had decreed that two-thirds of the members of the new legislative body must be elected from among the deputies who had sat in the Convention. This meant that the new body would be republican, in spite of the royalist revival that seemed to be in the making. P.-F. Réal describes the situation in Paris:

Paris had become the refuge of every conspirator, the hotbed of, the prime mover in, all conspiracies. Incorrigible royalism, ever defeated, ever optimistic, once more boldly raised its head. . . . A horde of Spaniards, Italians, Germans, English and Swiss, differing in dress, language and features, were the avowed agents of the vast conspiracy which was to devour France.

Members of the [old] Constituent and Legislative Assemblies, women, émigrés, and especially refractory priests, scattered and distributed throughout the several 'sections' of Paris, arranged gatherings, card parties and suppers at which, without any great attempt at concealment, preparations were made for the reduction, dissolution and massacre of the Convention, the proscription and massacre of all patriots, and the return of three or four kings who, seconded by three or four powers, were for another hundred years perhaps to deluge France with the blood of its unhappy inhabitants.

The rising was to take place on 13 vendémiaire [5 October 1795]. Just as, in the old days, the Faubourgs St-Antoine and St-Marcel had taken the lead in revolutionary activity, so in 1795 the richest district of Paris—the 'section' Le Pelletier—took the lead in counter-revolutionary, or royalist, activity. On 12 vendémiaire in the Convention, according to Baron Fain:

Time presses. A new general is needed. He is needed that very night. The issue has become so personal for the members of the Convention that they are no longer anxious to hand over the command of the troops to an outsider; this command must be entrusted to a representative, and all eyes turn towards the general of 9 thermidor. So it is that representative Barras is invested with the supreme command.

The new general has only the night in which to make his defensive dispositions. All the unemployed officers in Paris throng round him to receive his orders. He appoints them to the various outlying posts, but he needs a second-in-command whom he can trust in regard to professional details, one who can, without question, take things in at a glance. So he calls in young General Bonaparte. . . . He sends for him and has him accepted as his lieutenant. This reinforcement is made in the privacy of the committee; Barras alone is known as commander by the outside world. All orders are given in his name.

The Convention itself, which did not adjourn until five o'clock in the morning, meets again at noon; Barras just shows himself there in order to reassure his colleagues. 'Remain at your post,' he says to them. 'I am going to mine.'

Barras, according to his own account, conferred with his aide-de-camp over the weight of numbers:

'They are 40,000 against 4,000, granted [I said]. We shall make up the deficiency in numbers by our courage; a single discharge of grape fired in the air will suffice to strike terror in the ranks of our opponents, who will all of them fly if a few of them get their faces scratched. They are merely Pompey's dandies, afraid of having their faces spoiled.' Such was my plan in all its simplicity. And when I said to Bonaparte: 'We must centralize,' he fully grasped my intentions. . . .

What course were they going to adopt? Their commanders probably did not know themselves. Suddenly a few shots were fired from the most advanced battalion of the grenadiers of the [rebel] National Guard. Those of the line, whom Bonaparte had by my orders concealed in the building contiguous to the rue du Bac, spurred on by the sound of shooting, sprang up and opened fire. Although unable to judge whether this preliminary skirmish was planned or fortuitous, I saw in it the beginning of a general engagement in which we would certainly be overpowered by numbers.

I had a twelve-pounder gun under the walls of the Hôtel de Nesle, near the rue de Beaune. The gunners stood ready with lighted fuses. I gave the order to fire, and the first volley of grape mowed down some of the nearest

50] The whiff of grapeshot on 13 vendémiaire (5 October 179

National Guardsmen. The whole column wavered, and its recoil proved to me that it could not stand its ground. I therefore gave orders to keep up the firing, but to fire entirely in the air as it seemed to me that the noise would be sufficient to disperse the hostile phalanxes. It was enough, as I had anticipated, to lay low a few of the vanguard; all the rest scattered. . . .

Civil war is undoubtedly the worst of all political evils. But the picture presented by the chaotic defeat of these well-fleshed battalions—who left their arms, and even their coats, on the field of battle as they followed the example of their doughty chiefs—roused the brave defenders of the Convention to mirth.

Barras, whose two motivating forces were self-preservation and self-glorification, spent the rest of his long life wishing he had never heard of his young Corsican second-in-command, who stole all the glory on 13 vendémiaire:

As he has, since his subsequent appearances on the stage, arrogated to himself the leading role and the sole influence in everything, it is necessary that I should once more point out in precise terms what relates to him personally.

Bonaparte was neither more nor less than my aide-de-camp on 13 vendémiaire. I was mounted, he was on foot, and consequently could not follow me wherever I went. The only mission he received from me was to go to the Pont Royal, and return and report to me what was going on there. He did not give, and did not have the authority to give, any order on his own account. He was never at any point of attack except at the Carrousel, whence he did not stir; Brune was in command there.

I have not left out, however, the fact that he gave indication of a quick military perception when, pulling me by the coat and drawing me a few paces away from a position which would have exposed me to the first discharge, he said to me in an outburst of animation which was the product of the circumstances: 'All would be lost if you were killed. The drama hinges on you alone; there is no one who could take your place. What action are you going to take?' It was then that I ordered Brune to fire his cannon, and Bonaparte, pressing my hand, exclaimed: 'The republic is saved.'

The republic was saved for the speculators, the profiteers, the nouveaux riches *who soon emerged under the Directory. The affectations and dress of this new aristocracy offered food for satire to those who remembered the old* noblesse *with nostalgia. L.-S. Mercier, the Girondin who had managed to survive in spite of everything, describes them:*

What commotion is this? What woman is this who is preceded by shouts

51] The new rich replace the old *noblesse*. Paris revives

of applause? . . . Her lightweight tights, like the famous buckskins of the
Comte d'Artois—which four tall lackeys held in the air so that he might drop
into them in such a way that no wrinkles formed; from which, after being
clamped into them all day, he had to be released in the evening by being
lifted up in the same way and with even more effort—these feminine breeches,
I say, very tight although of silk, surpass even the famous buckskins in their
perfect fit. They are adorned with bracelets. The bodice is cleverly cut away,
and beneath an artistically painted veil there palpitate the reservoirs of
maternity. A chemise of transparent linen leaves on view legs and thighs
encircled with gold and diamond-studded hoops. . . . So little is left to remove
that I am not sure if true modesty would not gain by the raising of the
transparent veil.

This bold hussy was one of the merveilleuses. *The male equivalent, known as an*
incroyable, *wore a square-cut, ill-tailored coat very long in the waist, calf-length
breeches, a cravat 'like a cushion', and thin Turkish-style slippers. His hair was frizzed
and parted over the forehead, floated loose over the ears, and was tied in a plait behind.
He carried a knotted stick, and wore spectacles on his nose. 'And this', remarked
Mercier almost regretfully, 'is the day that follows the yesterday of Robespierre.'*

*These were the bright young things who restored Paris to a gay, if somewhat eccentric,
normality. The Terror was over, the revolution—if the political manœuvrings of the
Directory were anything to go by—was over. Had it all been worth it? It certainly did
not look like it to the mass of the people at the time. Some of them must have laughed
when it was decreed that designers for the Savonnerie carpet manufactury should not*

depict any human figures in their patterns, 'since it would be revolting to tread them underfoot under a government that has recalled Man to his dignity'.

And after the revolution? Empire.

In 1792, Robespierre had warned France: 'Put yourselves on guard even against the glory of your generals. . . . Watch, lest there arise in France a citizen so redoubtable that he one day becomes the master.' Within five years of this warning, the nation was on its knees worshipping a little Corsican general who had been suspended from his duties after thermidor for his Jacobin sympathies. Within ten years, this general had become the country's master. Within twelve years, he was its emperor.

As the men of the revolution had done, Napoleon led France to glory and to ruin. The ruin was measurable, and the glory was fleeting. France almost bled to death.

But the French revolution has never been effaced from men's minds. The image of 1789, the ideals of liberty and equality, were to send men of every colour and creed to the barricades in the fight against tyranny and oppression. History ceased to be the sole prerogative of kings, and ordinary people began to demand a say in their own destiny.

52] Bonaparte as first consul

Notes on the Quotations

The States-General

MORRIS, GOUVERNEUR (1752–1816) American statesman who was responsible for much of the final wording of the American constitution. He was in Europe from 1789 on, and was accredited as American minister in Paris between 1792 and 1794. His *Diary of the French Revolution* (published in 1889) is invaluable, but does not cover the sixteen months of the Terror.

BAILLY, JEAN-SYLVAIN (1736–94) Eminent French astronomer who became president of the National Assembly and then mayor of Paris. He lost popularity in 1791 when he permitted the National Guard to fire on republican petitioners at the Champ-de-Mars, and ended a victim of the guillotine. His *Memoirs* (edited Berville and Barrière, Paris, 1821) are partly based on the official minutes of the events they chronicle.

The Bastille Falls

YOUNG, ARTHUR (1741–1820) English writer and authority on farming. His *Annals of Agriculture* ran to forty-seven volumes, but he is better remembered today for his *Travels in France*, first published in London 1792.

DORSET, JOHN FREDERICK SACKVILLE, THIRD DUKE OF (1745–99) Britain's 'ambassador extraordinary' in France, 1783–89. His *Despatches from Paris 1784–90* were collected and published in 1909.

HUMBERT, JEAN-BAPTISTE (dates unknown) A Parisian clockmaker, who issued a pamphlet describing his experiences on the glorious 14 July: *The day of Jean-Baptiste Humbert, clockmaker, who was the first to climb on the towers of the Bastille* (Paris 1789)

La Bastille devoilée Nine issues of this periodical, which was published by Charpentier, appeared in 1789 and 1790. The second number contains eye-witness accounts by defenders of the Bastille.

RIGBY, EDWARD (1747–1821) A Norwich physician who visited Paris in the summer of 1789. His *Letters from France 1789* were published by his daughter, Lady Eastlake, in 1880.

The October Days

MAILLARD, STANISLAS (1763–*c*. 1795) After taking part in the fall of the Bastille, Maillard was prominent (and by no means innocent) during the events of October 1789. In 1792, he presided over the impromptu and bloody tribunal at the Abbaye Prison during the September massacres. He survived the revolution but died, apparently of tuberculosis, soon after. His description of the march to Versailles is taken from the evidence he gave at the Châtelet inquiry, which took place in 1790. It is printed as an appendix to the *Memoirs of Bailly* (see under 'The States-General', above).

Révolutions de Paris A weekly journal which was first published two days before the fall of the Bastille and survived for 225 issues, the last appearing on 28 February 1794. It took a radical line, and was edited by Elysée Loustallot and L.-M. Prudhomme. Our quotation is from issue no. XIII.

LA FAYETTE, MARIE-JEAN-PAUL etc. MARQUIS DE (1757–1834) An outstanding figure in the early part of the revolution. He believed in a constitutional monarchy; when the throne fell in August 1792, he fled to Austria. Our quotation is taken from a *Collection of Discourses* which he himself prepared in 1829 and which appeared in 1837 as part of the *Memoirs, Correspondence and Manuscripts of General La Fayette, published by his family.*

BLAIKIE, THOMAS (1750–1838) Scots landscape gardener and botanist who began his European travels in 1775 and was later employed by the Duc d'Orléans; he lived most of his adult life in France. Constant use of French had an uncanny but picturesque effect on his writing in English; extracts from his diary were published in 1931 as *Diary of a Scotch Gardener at the French Court*.

Interlude

DESMOULINS, CAMILLE (1762–94) Journalist, whose *Révolutions de France et de Brabant* (issue no. 34 is quoted here) was a lighter and more extreme version of the *Révolutions de Paris*. His later journal, *Le Vieux Cordelier*, demanded cessation of the Terror, and he went with Danton to the guillotine as a result.

Courrier de Provence A thrice-weekly periodical, originally edited by the friends of Mirabeau. Its first incarnation was as the *Etats-Généraux*; it then became *Lettres du Comte de Mirabeau à ses Comettants*; finally, after the fall of the Bastille, it adopted the name which it was to adhere to until it ceased publication in 1791. The issue quoted is no. CLXV.

MARAT, JEAN-PAUL (1744–93) Born in Switzerland but partly Spanish in origin. Travelled extensively in Europe and spent almost ten years in Britain, where he acquired a medical degree of the University of St Andrews. Returned to France and became a fashionable practitioner. Founded the extremist journal *l'Ami du Peuple* in 1789.

WELLESLEY-POLE, WILLIAM, later third Earl of Mornington (1763–1845) Brother of the Marquess Wellesley and the Duke of Wellington. At the time of his visit to France was British member of parliament for East Looe. He later held various govern-

ment posts and was a member of Lord Liverpool's Cabinet from 1814 to 1823.

The Flight to Varennes

ANGOULÊME, MARIE-THÉRÈSE-CHARLOTTE, DUCHESSE D' (1778–1851) Only daughter of Louis XVI and Marie Antoinette. Her parents and her aunt were guillotined, her two brothers died, her uncles fled the country. 'Madame Royale', as she was known, was the sole survivor of the Bourbons in France at the end of the revolution. She was deported in 1795 and four years later married her cousin, son of the Comte d'Artois (later Charles X). Bonaparte referred to her as 'the only man in the family'. Her account of the flight to Varennes was told in 1796 to Marie Antoinette's foster-brother, Weber, and printed in his memoirs, which were published in London in 1804–9.

LOUIS XVI (1754–93) King of France, grandson of Louis XV, succeeded to the throne in 1774. In 1770 he had been married to Marie Antoinette of Austria. It was one of history's more unsuitable matches—the stolid, kindly, stupid, devout young Bourbon, and the frivolous, unbiddable, autocratic daughter of the House of Hapsburg. Louis XVI's *Declaration of the King to all Frenchmen, on leaving Paris* is reproduced in L. G. Wickham Legg: *Select Documents illustrative of the History of the French Revolution* (Oxford 1905).

LEVESON-GOWER, GEORGE, first Duke of Sutherland (1758–1833) Succeeded Lord Dorset as ambassador to Paris in 1790. His *Despatches* were collected and published in 1885.

Politics in 1791

Révolutions de Paris See under 'The October Days', above.

Mercure de France A weekly journal, founded 1672, which before the revolution fulfilled the part of a court circular. Under the editorship of Mallet du Pan, it adopted a constitutional monarchist line which it maintained until the fall of the throne. The issue quoted is dated 24 September 1791.

WELLESLEY-POLE, WILLIAM See under 'Interlude', above.

REICHARDT, J. F. (1752–1814) German composer. At the age of twenty-three became Kapellmeister to Frederick II of Prussia. Visited Paris in 1785–86 and again in 1792. His letters from France were published in Berlin, 1792–93.

ROLAND DE LA PLATIÈRE, MARIE-JEANNE-PHLIPON, MADAME DE (1754–93) The wife of Jean Roland, minister of the interior during the period of Girondin supremacy. Mme Roland's influence was great with those susceptible to her charms, although by no means as extensive as is often suggested. But her intelligence was superior to that of most of the Girondins, and her *salon* was famous for a short and eventful period. Her comments are quoted from the Paris 1905 edition of the *Memoirs of Madame Roland*.

GRANDCHAMP, SOPHIE (dates unknown) A Parisian friend of Madame Roland, about whom little else is known. Her *Souvenirs* are included as an appendix to the Paris 1905 edition of the *Memoirs of Madame Roland*.

MILES, WILLIAM AUGUSTUS (1753–1807) English political writer, who lived in France from 1783 until 1791. His *Correspondence on the French Revolution* was published in 1890.

DESMOULINS, CAMILLE See under 'Interlude', above.

MERCIER, LOUIS-SÉBASTIEN (1740–1814) French author and dramatist, whose adaptations of Shakespeare left something to be desired. On social matters he was more penetrating and effective. He became a deputy in the Convention, allied himself

with the Girondins, and was imprisoned from 1793 until late 1794. His *Picture of Paris* (1783–88) provides a comprehensive view of the Paris scene; after the revolution, he published an equally comprehensive and didactic series entitled *The New Paris* (1797) from which our quotations are extracted.

The Revolution Goes to War

REICHARDT, J. F. See 'Politics in 1791', above.

ROBESPIERRE, MAXIMILIEN-MARIE-ISIDORE DE (1758–94) Born at Arras, where, after an education at the Louis-le-Grand College in Paris, he became an advocate. Was elected Third Estate representative for Arras in 1789. His consistency in an inconsistent society, his incorruptibility in a period when most men could be bought, gradually brought him to prominence. He was not a likeable personality, but the few friends he had were devoted to him. Bonaparte later said, with much truth, that Robespierre had been made the scapegoat of the revolution. His *Défenseur de la Constitution* was first issued in 1792.

The End of the Monarchy

TOURZEL, LOUISE-ELISABETH-FÉLICITÉ etc, MARQUISE DE (1748–1832) Governess to the children of France, 1789–92. After the attack on the Tuileries, was imprisoned in the Temple with the royal family for a short time, then removed to the Force Prison, where she narrowly escaped falling victim in the September massacres. Exiled during the empire; created a duchess at the restoration. The *Memoirs of the Duchess de Tourzel* were published in London in 1886.

BLAIKIE, THOMAS See under 'The October Days', above.

The September Massacres

RESTIF DE LA BRETONNE, NICOLAS-EDMÉ (1734–1806) Has been described as the 'first of the realists' in the modern sense. A writer whose impetuous, humanitarian, untidy work laid the foundations for Balzac and Maupassant. His *Monsieur Nicolas, Paris Nights* (1788) and *Revolutionary Nights* (1793) —from the last of which our quotations are taken—are the best remembered of his voluminous works.

WEBER, JOSEPH (1755–*c*. 1825) Born in Vienna; milk-brother to Marie Antoinette. Accompanied her to France as one of her valets-de-chambre. After his experiences during the September massacres, he escaped to England. His *Memoirs of Marie Antoinette* (London 1804–9) were partly written by Weber, partly by Lally-Tollendal.

In the Temple

MOORE, DR JOHN (1729–1802) Scots physician and occasional author, who published various accounts of his European travels. His *Journal during a Residence in France* (1793) is a valuable account of the last few months of 1792, when few foreigners remained in Paris.

A very strange report laid before the Commune *of Paris, concerning the enormous expenses of the prisoners in the Temple* This report (which is quoted from G. Lenôtre: *The Last Days of Marie Antoinette*, London 1907) was published in the form of a placard informing the citizens of Paris that, though they might be finding food dear, the prisoners in the Temple were feeding like fighting-cocks.

GORET, CHARLES (dates unknown) A former inspector of market supplies who became a member of the Paris *Commune*. Shortly after the restoration, he published *My testimony on the confinement of Louis XVI and his family in the Temple tower*.

TURGY, LOUIS-FRANÇOIS (1763–1823) Joined the staff of the royal kitchens at the age of twenty-one. After the restoration, was created an officer of the Légion d'Honneur and became first valet-de-

chambre to the Duchesse d'Angoulême (see under 'The Flight to Varennes', above). His narrative was published in 1818 as an appendix to the *Story of Louis XVII*, by Eckard.

ANGOULÊME, DUCHESSE D' See under 'The Flight to Varennes', above.

The Death of the King

YORKE, HENRY REDHEAD (1772–1813) Visited Paris as a young man of revolutionary sympathies, but was denounced and finally returned to England—where he was imprisoned as a spy from 1795 to 1798. His *Paris in 1802* includes recollections of his earlier visit.

MERCIER, LOUIS-SÉBASTIEN See under 'Politics in 1791', above.

MILLINGEN, JOHN GIDEON (1782–1862) Was in Paris with his father, who held a position at the Paris Mint in 1790–92. His *Recollections of Republican France* (1848) must owe much to later imagination, but it is perfectly possible that the atmosphere of the capital on the day of the king's death should have impressed itself truthfully on his child's mind.

EDGEWORTH, HENRY ESSEX, ABBÉ DE FIRMONT (1745–1807) Born in Ireland, but taken to live in France when only three years old. After the outbreak of the revolution, he became confessor to Madame Elisabeth, the king's sister, and later attended the king on his journey to the guillotine. He left France in 1796, and spent the last ten years of his life in the service of the exiled heir to the throne, Louis XVIII. His account of the execution of Louis XVI is included in *A Journal of the Terror* (London, Folio Society, 1955).

The Triumph of the Mountain

RESTIF DE LA BRETONNE See under 'The September Massacres', above.

PAINE, THOMAS (1737–1809) Although he had a talent for alienating the people with whom he came into personal contact, Paine had considerable influence as a writer. He served in the American army, returned to England in 1787 and published his *Rights of Man* (1790–92), as a result of which he had to flee to France. There, after enjoying some popularity, he was imprisoned for most of the year 1794. Disgusted with the Directory and Consulate, he returned to America in 1802 where he soon found himself at odds with society yet again. His letter to Danton is quoted in Conway's *Life of Paine*.

PÉTION DE VILLENEUVE, JÉROME (1753–94) Mayor of Paris, defeating La Fayette in the election for the post, from 1791 to 1792. Except for this period, he was a representative in the assemblies from 1789 until proscribed with the rest of the Girondin leaders in 1793. The quotation comes from the *Memoirs of Pétion* (Paris 1866), written while he was in hiding during the last months of his life.

LANJUINAIS, JEAN-DENIS (1753–1827) An advocate from Rennes who became a Girondin deputy. He was proscribed in 1793, but survived to become a peer of France on the restoration and president of the chamber of representatives in 1815. His description of 2 June is quoted in the anti-Jacobin pamphlet published in 1793 by A.-J. Gorsas (a Girondin deputy who did not share his colleague's good fortune, and went to the guillotine in October 1793), entitled *Brisk summary of the events which took place in Paris on the 30 and 31 May, 1 and 2 June 1793*

The Beginning of the End

SANSON, CHARLES-HENRI (1740–93) The public executioner of Paris, who was succeeded by his son, Henri (1767–1840). The *Memoirs of Sanson, contributing to the history of the Revolution* (Paris 1829) were the invention of Balzac and Lhéritier, though they may have been based on notes actually left by the executioner.

GUELLARD, JACQUES-PHILIBERT (dates unknown) Police superintendent of the Théâtre-Français section of Paris. The record of his preliminary interrogation of Charlotte Corday is in the Archives Nationales, Paris.

CORDAY D'ARMONT, MARIANNE-CHARLOTTE DE (1768–93) A descendant of the poet Corneille, well educated, full of ideals, but brought up without sophistication so that she still thought it possible for a single grand gesture to solve the complexities of revolutionary politics. Charlotte Corday's letter to her father is preserved in the Archives Nationales, Paris.

KLAUSE (dates unknown) German historian. His story of the last days of Charlotte Corday was published in Altona, 1793, as *Corday: A Trial*.

The Last Days of Marie Antoinette

LAMORLIÈRE, ROSALIE (c. 1773–c. 1845) A chambermaid, Rosalie could neither read nor write, but she told her story to Lafont d'Aussonne when he was engaged on a life of Marie Antoinette. The account also appears in *Marie Antoinette's Captivity in the Conciergerie* (Paris 1897).

CHAUVEAU-LAGARDE, CLAUDE-FRANÇOIS (1756–1841) A lawyer who was chosen to defend various star prisoners— including Brissot and Charlotte Corday— who had no hope of acquittal. His *Historical Note on the Trial of Marie Antoinette* was published in Paris, 1816.

Annual Register As its name suggests, a yearly publication devoted to the events of the preceding year. The first issue appeared in 1759, and the first editor was Edmund Burke. The *Annual Register* still exists today.

The Committee of Public Safety

Observers' reports Between March 1793 and March 1794, the ministry of the interior had a 'public opinion office' serviced by reports sent in daily by a dozen 'observers'. Many of these reports are quoted in J. G. Alger: *Paris in 1789–94* (London 1902).

LEVASSEUR, RENÉ (1747–1834) Surgeon, deputy in the National Convention. His description of the fall of Danton is reprinted in Alfred Bougeart: *Danton* (Brussels 1861).

VILATE, JOACHIM (1768–95) Member of the revolutionary tribunal. While imprisoned after thermidor, he recorded the *Secret Causes of the 9th and 10th Thermidor* in which he tried to excuse his own conduct. The quotation used comes from the third part of this work, subtitled *The Mysteries of the Mother of God revealed* (1795).

DAVID, JACQUES-LOUIS (1748–1825) The most influential artist of the revolution and empire. His genius for theatrical effect made him the ideal designer and producer of the fêtes which played so large a part in the social life of the revolution. After a few months in prison during the thermidorian reaction, he was restored to favour and finally became official painter to Bonaparte. Exiled after the restoration, he spent his last years in Belgium. His plan for the Fête of the Supreme Being is reprinted in the *Parliamentary History of the French Revolution 1789–1815* by P.-J.-B. Buchez and P.-C. Roux (Paris 1837).

The Terror

CODRINGTON, SIR WILLIAM (*c.* 1765–1816) Disinherited by his father, Codrington was resident in France and was arrested as an enemy alien on the outbreak of war with Britain. After his release, he wrote an account of his experiences to friends in London. His letter is reproduced in J. G. Alger: *Englishmen in the French Revolution* (London 1889).

BEUGNOT, JACQUES-CLAUDE, COMTE DE (1761–1835) A lawyer, deputy to the Legislative Assembly. Later became a minister to Bonaparte, then to Louis XVIII. His *Memoirs 1785–1815* were published in Paris, 1866.

CARRICHON, THE ABBÉ (dates unknown) A 'refractory' priest, i.e. one who did not subscribe to the civil constitution of the clergy. His description of the execution of the Noailles ladies was published in the *Nouvelle Revue*, January–February 1888.

KERVERSEAU, F.-M. DE (dates unknown) Part author with Clavelin of a *History of the French Revolution of 1789 by two friends of Liberty* (Paris 1790–1803).

The Fall of Robespierre

ROBESPIERRE, CHARLOTTE DE (1760–1834) Sister of Maximilien and Augustin, for whom she kept house in Paris for a short time. She survived the anti-Jacobin reaction after the revolution. The passages quoted are from the Paris 1910 edition of *Charlotte Robespierre's memoirs of her two brothers.*

FOUCHÉ, JOSEPH, DUC D'OTRANTE (1759–1820) A renegade churchman, who— misreading the true political situation—was over-zealous in applying the rule of Terror at Lyon. His instinct for survival served him well, however, and he later became one of Bonaparte's most rewarded lieutenants. Again he misjudged the situation in 1810 when, foreseeing the downfall of Bonaparte, he began secret negotiations with the exiled Bourbons. His *Memoirs* (Paris 1824) were disowned by his scandalized descendants and it is only in recent years that historians have come to regard them as at least partially authentic.

MÉDA, CHARLES-ANDRÉ (1774–1812) After his moment of fame in 1794, Méda (or Merda, or Médal) spent almost ten years demanding his reward for saving the nation. He won military advancement during the reign of Bonaparte, becoming 'baron of the empire' in 1808, but died of wounds during Bonaparte's Russian campaign. His *Historical Summary of the Events which took place during the evening of 9 Thermidor* was written in 1802 and published in Paris, 1825.

COURTOIS, EDMÉ-BONAVENTURE (1754–1816) Deputy of the Convention, who was responsible for producing an official report on the events of 9 thermidor. Parts of this report are reprinted in the *Parliamentary History of the French Revolution 1789–1815* by P.-J.-B. Buchez and P.-C. Roux (Paris 1837).

The Whiff of Grapeshot

RÉAL, PIERRE-FRANÇOIS, COMTE DE (1757–1834) One of Bonaparte's life councillors. His *Essay on the days of 13 and 14 vendémiaire* was published in Paris, 1796.

FAIN, AGATHON-JEAN-FRANÇOIS, BARON (1778–1836) Secretary to the Directory and, later, to Bonaparte. His manuscript record of the events of vendémiaire, written in 1795, is reprinted in *Memoirs of Barras* edited by George Duruy (London, translation, 1895).

BARRAS, PAUL JEAN FRANÇOIS NICOLAS, VICOMTE DE (1755–1829) After an early military career, was elected as a deputy to the Convention. Became one of the five members of the Directory, but the advent of Bonaparte ended his political career. There is an English translation of his *Memoirs*, edited by George Duruy (London 1895).

MERCIER, LOUIS-SEBASTIÉN See under 'Politics in 1791', above.

Notes on the Illustrations

The present location or source of the illustrations is shown in italics at the end of each entry. The publishers gratefully acknowledge the permission to reproduce granted by the galleries and collections concerned.

1] Louis XVI by Joseph-Silfrède Duplessis (1725–1802), who was created director of the royal galleries at Versailles in 1780. He specialized in portraiture but also painted a few landscapes with figures. *Musée de Versailles.*

2] Fête by night at the Petit Trianon. A painting by Claude-Louis Chatelet, specialist in pastoral scenes. Born in 1753, he became an ardent republican, served on the revolutionary tribunal, and was condemned to death for it after thermidor, being guillotined on 6 May 1795. *Musée Carnavalet, Paris.*

3] Opening of the States-General. A plate engraved by Isidore Stanislas Helman (1743–1809) after an original by the narrative painter Charles Monnet (1732–c. 1808) for the series *Principal Days of the Revolution*. Illustration no. 41 is by the same two artists. *Mansell Collection, London.*

4] The Oath of the Tennis Court. Bailly stands on the table, the Abbé Sieyès is seated beside it, and the third full-length figure beyond him to the right is Robespierre (it is not clear why he should be beating his breast in such a distracted fashion). The original painting is by Jacques-Louis David (1748–1825), the outstanding artist of the revolution and empire, who also acted as designer and producer of the spectaculars which played such an important part in revolutionary propaganda. The aquatint version shown here is by Jean-Pierre-Marie

Jazet (1788–1871), nephew and pupil of the celebrated engraver, Debucourt (see 29, below). *By courtesy of the Trustees of the British Museum.*

5] Freedom of the press. An anonymous colour print showing one of the printing workshops which did such enormous business in the early part of the revolution. *Bibliothèque Nationale, Paris.*

6] The fall of the Bastille. Oil painting, artist unknown. *Musée de Versailles.*

7] The market-women march to Versailles. Engraved by Berthault—probably Pierre-Gabriel (1748–1819)—after an original by Prieur. Prieur is something of a headache to art historians, but it seems likely that he was born about 1759 and that he perished by the guillotine either in 1793, or in 1795 at the same time and for the same reason as Chatelet (see 2, above). The plate comes from the *Complete Collection of Pictures of Historic Events of the French Revolution* (Paris 1802).

8] The heads of the two bodyguards brought back from Versailles. A contemporary colour print, anonymous. *By courtesy of the Trustees of the British Museum.*

9] The tree of liberty. The planting of young oaks and poplars was a charming piece of symbolism taken over from the May Day ceremony of the *ancien régime*. By mid 1792, over sixty thousand had been planted throughout France, although both trees and liberty frequently wilted in the care of men unaccustomed to handling them. The illustration is a gouache by Pierre-Étienne Lesueur, whose dates are unknown but who exhibited at the Salon between 1791 and 1810. *Musée Carnavalet, Paris.*

10] Marie Antoinette and her family; the elder of the two boys, the first dauphin, died in 1789. The portrait is by Madame Marie-Louise-Elisabeth Vigée-Lebrun (1755–1842), one of the world's most successful women artists. Wisely, she left France in October 1789, and spent the next thirteen years in Italy, Austria, and Russia. *Musée de Versailles.*

11] The royal family arrested during supper at Varennes. Engraved by Berthault after Prieur, for the *Complete Collection . . .* (see 7, above).

12] The royal family re-enters Paris. A contemporary colour print, anonymous. *Bibliothèque Nationale, Paris.*

13] Brissot. Anonymous portrait. *Musée Carnavalet, Paris.*

14] Vergniaud. Drawing by Duranceau (dates unknown). *Musée Lambinet, Versailles.*

15] Condorcet. Portrait, school of Greuze. *Musée de Versailles.*

16] Madame Roland. Portrait by Johann or Jean Heinsius (1740–1812), a German artist who had some success at the French court before the revolution. *Musée de Versailles.*

17] Robespierre. Drawing by Jacques-Louis David (see 4, above). *Private collection.*

18] Danton. An engraving by Sandoz (? Ulysse, 1788–1815) after an original by the late-eighteenth-century portraitist and engraver, François Bonneville, who edited and in most cases engraved the plates for a four-volume work of *Portraits of the celebrated personalities of the Revolution* (Paris 1793–1802).

19] Saint-Just. Anonymous drawing. *Musée Carnavalet, Paris.*

20] Marat. Portrait by Joseph Boze (1744–1826). An artist with a talent for catching a resemblance on canvas. He was ingenious enough to be popular at the court of Louis XVI, then with the revolutionaries, then with Bonaparte, and finally with Louis XVIII after the restoration. *Musée Carnavalet, Paris.*

21 and 22] A *sans-culotte* and his wife. Anonymous colour print, contemporary. *Bibliothèque Nationale, Paris.*

23] Announcement of war with Austria in the Jacobin club. A contemporary caricature showing Dumouriez, the leading figure in the king's Girondin ministry and one of those most firmly committed to war, wearing the appearance of a goose. *Bibliothèque Nationale, Paris.*

24] The departure of the volunteer. Painting by François-Louis-Joseph Watteau (1758–1823), known as Watteau de Lille. *Musée Carnavalet, Paris.*

25] Attack on the Tuileries. Painting by an artist who alternated between scenes of battle and pastoral bliss, Jacques Bertaux (dates unknown). This painting was finished in time to be exhibited at the Salon of 1793. *Musée de Versailles.*

26] The crowd invades the assembly. Pen design by François-Pascal-Simon Gérard (1770–1837), narrative and portrait painter, a pupil of David (see 4, above). Like David, he was very successful during the empire, but unlike him Gérard survived the restoration. He was created a baron in 1819. *Musée du Louvre, Paris.*

27] Massacre at the Salpétrière on 3 September 1792. An engraving from Prudhomme's periodical *Révolutions de Paris* (see Notes on the Quotations, under 'The October Days'). *Bibliothèque Nationale, Paris.*

28] The end of the Princesse de Lamballe. An anonymous engraving of the period from the *Gentleman's Magazine*. *Bibliothèque Nationale, Paris.*

29] The public promenade at the Palais Royal, a great social centre both before, and during the first part of, the revolution. When the Duc d'Orléans became known as Philippe-Egalité, the Palais Royal became known as the Palais Egalité. Colour print by Louis-Philibert Debucourt (1755–1832), who was originally a genre painter but gave it up in 1785 to concentrate on aquatinting. His reputation in this medium was, and is, pre-eminent. *Bibliothèque Nationale, Paris.*

30] The royal family at dinner in the Temple. Contemporary engraving, anonymous. *Musée Carnavalet, Paris.*

31] Louis XVI in the Temple, three days before his execution. Pencil drawing on tinted paper, heightened with white, by Joseph Ducreux (1737–1802). In 1769, Ducreux had been sent to Austria to paint a portrait of Marie-Antoinette for her intended bridegroom. His reputation was thus established, and he painted many notable portraits thereafter. *Musée Carnavalet, Paris.*

32] The king bids farewell to his family and retainers. *Left to right:* the Abbé Edgeworth; Marie Antoinette; Madame Royale (later Duchesse d'Angoulême); Louis XVI; the dauphin (Louis XVII, after his father's death); Madame Elisabeth (the king's sister); and the valet, Cléry. The original painting is by Charles Benazech (1767–1794) who was born in London but worked with Greuze in Paris; many engravings, by many hands, were made from this original. *Musée de Versailles.*

33] The execution of the king. Anonymous colour print. *Musée Carnavalet, Paris.*

34] Decree of the National Convention, 6 April 1793, setting up the Committee of Public Safety which was effectively to rule France from mid 1793 until after the fall of Robespierre in July 1794. *Archives Nationales, Paris.*

35] Hérault de Séchelles attempts to lead the members of the Convention out of the hall on 2 June 1793, and finds himself opposed by Hanriot. Anonymous engraving after an original by Fulchran-Jean Harriet (b. ?–1805), who worked in the studio of David (see 4, above) and exhibited at the Louvre between 1796 and 1802. *Bibliothèque Nationale, Paris.*

36] Marat assassinated. One of the most famous subjects painted by David (see 4, above). *Musée de Versailles.*

37] The arrest of Charlotte Corday, whom artistic licence presents as an ethereal blonde. She was in fact of sturdy build and brunette colouring. This is a wash drawing by Louis-Leopold Boilly (1761–1845), a prolific artist with an inquiring mind and an experimental hand. He was denounced during the revolution, but survived to continue painting until the age of eighty-three. *Musée Lambinet, Versailles.*

38] Arrest of a suspect. Watercolour by Béricourt, a late-eighteenth-century artist who specialized in this medium. *Musée Carnavalet, Paris.*

39] 'The widow Capet at the Conciergerie.' An oil sketch by Prieur (see 7, above). *Musée Carnavalet, Paris.*

40] The interrogation of Marie Antoinette. The public prosecutor, Fouquier-Tinville, is on the extreme left of the picture. Engraved after an original by Pierre Bouillon (1776–1831), a painter and engraver who exhibited at the Salon in 1796. *Mansell Collection, London.*

41] Execution of Marie Antoinette, engraved by Helman after an original by Monnet (see 3, above). *Photo Bulloz, Mansell Collection, London.*

42] Condorcet poisons himself in prison, April 1794. Engraved by Berthault for the *Complete Collection* . . . (see 7, above), after an original by Alexandre-Evariste Fragonard (1780–1850), known as Fragonard fils. He was the pupil of his more famous father, and of David (see 4, above), and his work in the field of historical illustration began to appear as early as 1795.

43] The Fête of the Supreme Being at the Champ-de-Mars. The symbolic Mountain with its tree of liberty is clearly visible in the background. The painting is by Pierre-Antoine Demachy (1723–1807) whose great talent was for architectural and narrative or historical scenes. *Musée Carnavalet, Paris.*

44] A revolutionary committee under the Terror. Engraved by Berthault for the *Complete Collection* . . . (see 7, above), after an original by Fragonard fils (see 42, above).

45] 'The last prayer of Madame Anne Elisabeth.' Engraved by Silanio (about whom nothing is known) after an original by Pellegrini (probably Domenico, the eighteenth- to nineteenth-century portraitist). *By courtesy of the Trustees of the British Museum.*

46] 'Loizerolles gives up his life for his son.' Engraved by Berthault for the *Complete Collection* . . . (see 7, above) after an original by Jean Duplessis-Bertaux (1747–1813 or 1818), a topographical and narrative artist who was himself also a very fine engraver.

47] 'The last victims of the Terror are called.' The seated figure in the centre foreground is André Chénier, the poet, who was executed two days before the fall of Robespierre. This is the only one of our illustrations which is not a contemporary work. It is, however, so familiar and so evocative that its inclusion seems justifiable. The artist was Charles-Louis-Lucien Müller (1815–92), a portraitist and genre painter whose reputation was great during his lifetime. 'The last call' was exhibited at the Salon of 1850. *Musée de Versailles.*

48] 'Robespierre guillotining the executioner after having had the whole of France guillotined.' A typical engraving of the period which followed thermidor. Anonymous print. *Musée Carnavalet, Paris.*

49] The arrest of Robespierre. Engraved by Michael Sloane (early nineteenth century, English, a pupil of Bartolozzi) after an original by Barbier. There were at least six painters named Barbier working at this time; it seems likely that the artist concerned here was G.-P. Barbier, who worked in London and exhibited many portraits at the Royal Academy between 1792 and 1795. *By courtesy of the Trustees of the British Museum.*

50] 'Attack by the National Convention.' Engraved by Berthault for the *Complete Collection* . . . (see 7, above) after an original by Abraham Girardet (1764–1823), a Swiss designer and engraver who worked in France for many years.

51] The Pavillon de Hanovre, at the corner of the boulevard des Italiens and the rue Louis-le-Grand. Anonymous drawing, colour, *c*. 1795. *Bibliothèque Nationale, Paris.*

52] 'The First Consul.' One of the most impressive works David (see 4, above) ever produced. Experts on the anatomy of the horse are withering in their criticisms of Bonaparte's charger, but the colour and construction of the portrait have an impact which is wholly dynamic. Contrast this picture of the first consul crossing the Alps with Duplessis's portrait of Louis XVI on page 10, and it becomes clear that the revolution did achieve something—even if it was not what the revolutionaries expected. *Musée de Versailles.*

The title page border is from *Révolutions de Paris*, Paris 1789.

The extracts from *The Diary of a Scotch Gardener at the French court at the end of the eighteenth century* by Thomas Blaikie (ed. F. Birrell, 1931) are published by kind permission of Routledge and Kegan Paul Ltd. The translations of the stories by Comte Beugnot (page 99), the Abbé Carrichon (page 100), and F.-M. de Kerverseau (page 101) are by Richard Graves, and are reproduced from *The French Revolution* by Georges Pernoud and Sabine Flaissier, by kind permission of Secker and Warburg Ltd.